2A

World Class

EXPANDING ENGLISH FLUENCY

NANCY DOUGLAS | JAMES R. MORGAN

NATIONAL GEOGRAPHIC LEARNING | CENGAGE Learning®

Australia • Brazil • Japan • Korea • Mexico • Singapore • Spain • United Kingdom • United States

NATIONAL GEOGRAPHIC LEARNING | CENGAGE Learning

World Class: Expanding English Fluency
Student Edition
Nancy Douglas and James R. Morgan

Publisher: Sherrise Roehr
Managing Editor: Sarah Thérèse Kenney
Development Editors: Michael Poor, Michael Tom
Senior Technology Product Manager: Scott Rule
Technology Project Manager: Chris Conroy
Director of Global Marketing: Ian Martin
Senior Product Marketing Manager: Katie Kelley
Director, Content and Media Production: Michael Burggren
Content Project Manager: Andrea Bobotas
Print Buyer: Mary Beth Hennebury
Cover Designer: Cenveo Publisher Services
Cover Image: Chris Brundige
Compositor: Cenveo Publisher Services

Student Book + Student CD-ROM ISBN: 978-1-133-56589-5
Student Book + Online Workbook ISBN: 978-1-285-06308-9
Combo Split 2A + Student CD-ROM ISBN: 978-1-133-56590-1
Combo Split 2A + Online Workbook ISBN: 978-1-285-41989-3

National Geographic Learning
20 Channel Center Street
Boston, MA 02210
USA

Cengage Learning is a leading provider of customized learning solutions with office locations around the globe, including Singapore, the United Kingdom, Australia, Mexico, Brazil and Japan.

Cengage Learning products are represented in Canada by Nelson Education, Ltd.

Visit National Geographic Learning online at **ngl.cengage.com**

Visit our corporate website at **www.cengage.com**

Photo Credits

Unit 1 **pp.x–1**: Tim Pannell/Corbis; **p.2**: Cindy Hughes/Shutterstock.com; **p.4**: Rachel Frank/Corbis; **p.5**: Digital Vision/Thinkstock; **p.6**: Christopher Pillitz/In Pictures/Corbis; **p.7**: Randy Olson/National Geographic Stock; **p.8**: UIG via Getty Images; **p.11**: D. Hurst/Alamy

Unit 2 **p.12–13**: Marin Tomaš/Demotix/Corbis; **p.14** left: PhotoAlto/Alamy, right: Tomas Rodriguez/Corbis; **p.15**: Chris Collins/Corbis; **p.16** top: Andre van der Veen/Shutterstock.com, bottom: ©iStockphoto.com/97; **p.17**: Michael Melford/National Geographic Stock; **p.18**: ©iStockphoto.com/drbimages; **p.19** top: Karen Kasmauski/Corbis, bottom: Atlantide Phototravel/Corbis; **p.20**: Datacraft Co., Ltd./Corbis; **p.21** Tetra Images/Corbis; **p.23**: Image Source/Corbis

Unit 3 **pp.24–25**: Songquan Deng/Shutterstock.com; **p.26**: Murat Taner/Getty Images; **p.27**: Kazuko Kimizuka/Getty Images; **p.28**: Paulo Fridman/Corbis; **p.29** top: Atlantide Phototravel/Corbis, below: Aaron Amat/Shutterstock.com; **p.31**: Greg Girard/National Geographic Stock; **p.32** top & below: MORANDI Bruno/Hemis/Corbis; **p.34**: Florian Werner/Getty Images; **p.35** top & bottom: Jane Sweeney/JAI/Corbis

Unit 4 **pp.36–37**: Radius Images/Corbis; **p.38** top: Brooke Whatnall/National Geographic Stock, bottom: Kimberly White/Reuters/Corbis; **p.39**: vipflash/Shutterstock.com; **p.40**: Frederic Cirou/PhotoAlto/Corbis; **p.41**: Zigy Kaluzny–Charles Thatcher/Getty Images; **p.43**: Topic Photo Agency/Corbis; **p.44**: David Sutherland/Getty Images; **p.45**: Lawrence Manning/Corbis; **p.46**: Tim Pannell/Corbis; **p.47** top: Rubberball/Mike Kemp, bottom: Ocean/Corbis

Unit 5 **pp.48–49**: Agustin Esmoris/National Geographic My Shot; **p.50** top: Arman Taylo/National Geographic My Shot, below: Mitsuaki Iwago/Minden Pictures; **p.51**: Tim Fitzharris/Minden Pictures; **p.52**: Ewan Burns/Corbis; **p.53**: Department for International Development; **p.54** left: Richard Nowitz/National Geographic Stock, right: Ocean/Corbis; **p.55**: National Geographic Maps/National Geographic Image Collection; **p.56** top: Atlaspix/Shutterstock.com, below: Layne Kennedy/Corbis; **pp.56–57**: Kenneth Geiger/National Geographic Stock; **p.59** left: Christoph Gerigk ©Franck Goddio/Hilti Foundation, right: Sergey Kamshylin/Shutterstock.com, donatas1205/Shutterstock.com

Unit 6 **pp.60–61**: Image Source/Corbis; **p.62** top: Kirsty Wigglesworth/AP/Corbis, bottom: Oliver Killig/epa/Corbis; **p.64**: MCT via Getty Images; **p.65**: Peter Ginter/Science Faction/Corbis; **p.66**: NASA; **p.67**: Art by Stefan Morrell. Sources: Christopher McKay, NASA Ames Research Center; James Graham, University of Wisconsin -Madison; Robert Zubrin, Mars Society; Margarita Marinova, California Institute of Technology. Earth and Mars images: NASA; **p.69**: NASA – digital version copyright/Science Faction/Corbis; **p.70** top: Maria Stenzel/National Geographic Stock, bottom: Tyrone Turner/National Geographic Stock; **p.71**: Sigrid Olsson/PhotoAlto/Corbis

Text Credits

Readings from the following units were adapted from National Geographic.

Unit 1 Adapted from *What Happens When a Language Dies?* by Paroma Basu, National Geographic Extreme Explorer, February 26, 2009. **Unit 2** Adapted from *Nobel Peace Prize Goes to Micro-Loan Pioneers* by Stefan Lovgren, National Geographic Traveler, October 13, 2006. **Unit 3** Adapted from *The City Solution* by Robert Kunzig, National Geographic Magazine, December 2011. **Unit 4** Adapted from *Secrets of the Happiest Places on Earth* by Ford Cochran, National Geographic NewsWatch, November 22, 2010. **Unit 5** Adapted from *Bejeweled Stonehenge Boy Came From Mediterranean?* by Kate Ravilious, National Geographic News, October 13, 2010. **Unit 6** Adapted from *Making Mars the New Earth* by *Robert Kunzig*, National Geographic Magazine, January 15, 2010 and *Q&A: Robert Zubrin, Mars Pathfinder* by Ted Chamberlain, National Geographic ADVENTURE, September/October, 2000.

Printed in China
3 4 5 6 7 23 22 21 20 19

Acknowledgements

The authors and editorial team would like to thank the many dedicated instructors who took the time to review World Class. *Their feedback was invaluable during the development of this program.*

UNITED STATES Touria Ghaffari, EC New York, New York, New York; **Olga Gusak,** Computer Systems Institute, Skokie, Illinois; **William Jex,** American Language Institute, New York University, New York, New York; **Bridget McDonald,** Independent Learning Services, Boston, Massachusetts; **Saida Pagan,** North Valley OC, Mission Hills, California; **Tara Tarpey,** American Language Institute, New York University, New York, New York

LATIN AMERICA Luiz Otávio Barros, Associação Alumni, Brazil; **Clarissa Bezerra,** Casa Thomas Jefferson, Brazil; **Isabela Villas Boas,** Casa Thomas Jefferson, Brazil; **Tatiane C. de Carvalho,** Cultura Britânica e Americana, Brazil; **Rafael Reis Carpanez,** Cultura Inglesa, Brazil; **Janette Carvalhinho de Oliveira,** Centro de Linguas - UFES, Brazil; **Samara Camilo Tomé Costa,** IBEU, Brazil; **Frank Couto,** Casa Thomas Jefferson, Brazil; **Denise Santos da Silva,** Associação Cultural Estados Unidos, Brazil; **Marilena Fernandes,** Associação Alumni, Brazil; **Vanessa Ferreira,** Associação Cultural Brasil Estados Unidos, Brazil; **Marcia Ferreira,** CCBEU Franca, Brazil; **Maria Regina Filgueiras,** College Language Center, Brazil; **Maria Righini,** Associação Cultura Inglesa, Brazil; **Bebeth Silva Costa,** Betina's English Course, Brazil; **Domingos Sávio Siqueira,** Federal University of Bahia, Brazil; **Joyce von Söhsten,** English by Joyce von Söhsten, Brazil; **Doris Flores,** Universidad Santo Tomas, Chile; **Sandra Herrera,** Inacap Apoquindo, Chile; **Jair Ayala Zarate,** La Salle University, Colombia; **Rosario Mena,** Instituto Cultural Dominico Americano, Dominican Republic; **Raúl Billini,** Language Program Administration, Dominican Republic; **Rosa Vásquez,** John F. Kennedy Institute of Languages, INC., Dominican Republic; **Elizabeth Ortiz,** COPEI-COPOL English Institute, Ecuador; **José Alonso Gaxiola Soto,** Universidad Autonoma de Sinaloa, Mexico; **María Elena Mesías Ratto,** Universidad de San Martín de Porres, Peru

EUROPE AND THE MIDDLE EAST Juan Irigoyen, International Institute, Spain; **Nashwa Nashaat Sobhy,** San Jorge University, Spain; **Barbara Van der Veer,** International Institute, Spain; **Deborah Wilson,** American University of Sharjah, United Arab Emirates

ASIA Michael Lay, American Intercon Institute, Cambodia; **Kirkland Arizona Kenney,** Beijing New Oriental School, China; **Isao Akama,** Waseda University, Japan; **Benjamin Bailey,** University of Shizuoka, Japan; **James Baldwin,** Tokyo University of Agriculture and Technology, Japan; **Jonathan deHaan,** University of Shizuoka, Japan; **Todd Enslen,** Tohoku University, Japan; **Peter Gray,** Hokusei Gakuen University, Japan; **Linda Hausman,** Gakushuin University, Japan; **Mauro Lo Dico,** Nanzan University, Japan; **Nobue Mori,** Kumamoto Gakuen University, Japan; **Yuri Nishio,** Gifu Pharmaceutical University, Japan; **Geraldine Norris,** The Prefectual University of Shizuoka, Japan; **Christopher Piper,** Takushoku University, Japan; **Michael Radcliffe,** Yokohama City University, Japan; **Jean-Pierre Richard,** Kanagawa University, Sophia University, Japan; **Greg Rouault,** Konan University, Hirao School of Management, Japan; **Stephen Ryan,** Yamagata University, Japan; **Gregory Strong,** Aoyama Gakuin University, Japan; **Michael Yasui,** Tokyo Metropolitan University, Japan; **Sun Mi Ma,** Ajou University, Korea; **Palarak Chaiyo,** Rajamangala University of Technology Suvarnabhumi, Thailand; **Krishna Kosashunhanan,** Thai-Nichi Institute of Technology, Thailand; **Jonee de Leon,** Universal English Center, Vietnam; **Ai Nguyen Huynh Thi,** VUS, Vietnam

We would also like to extend a special thank-you to Yeny Kim for her many insights. Her thoughtful contributions were a great asset and will be felt by students and teachers alike.

	UNIT	VOCABULARY	GRAMMAR	LISTENING
UNIT 1	 Language and Life, 1	How do you communicate?	Quantifiers	Lecture on communicating effectively **Strategy:** Listening for definitions **Pronunciation:** Stress on content words versus function words
UNIT 2	 Money Talks, 12	Your spending habits	Noun Clauses	Two big purchases: Are they worth it? **Strategy:** Expressing an opinion (with Connections)
UNIT 3	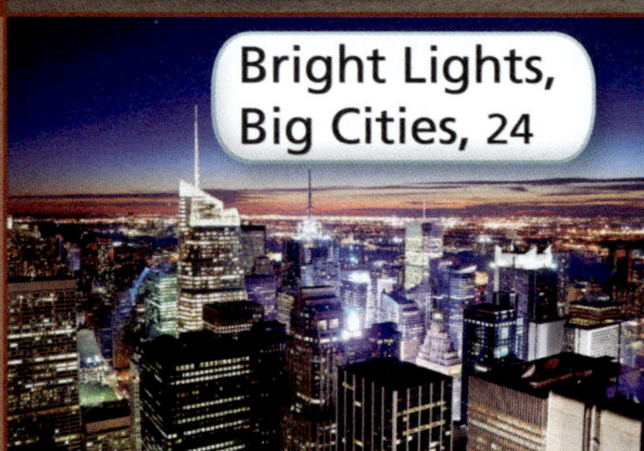 Bright Lights, Big Cities, 24	Cities of the world quiz	Dynamic and Stative Passive	A trip to a "green" city
UNIT 4	 Being Yourself, 36	Daredevil or philosopher: What are you like?	Making Wishes	A challenging lab partner
UNIT 5	 Mystery Solved!, 48	Animal mysteries	Modals of Possibility in the Past, Present, and Future	A news story about a miraculous rescue
UNIT 6	 New Horizons, 60	Robot revolution	Predictions with Future Forms	The future of air travel **Strategy:** Signal phrases

	READING	WRITING	SPEAKING	VIDEO
	What Happens When a Language Dies?: Languages disappearing worldwide **Strategy:** Working with restatement questions	Write a report summary **Strategy:** Writing a report summary	Present your report summary **Strategy:** Interpreting the results and questioning the results	*A Hidden Language Recorded*
	Micro Loans, Macro Impact **Strategy:** Determine the meaning of unfamiliar words in a text	Write about advantages and disadvantages	Convince a billionaire investor to loan you money	*Borrowing Money*
	Rapid Urbanization: A case study **Strategy:** Locating and reading statistics	Write a summary **Strategy:** Guidelines on summary writing	Talk about push/pull factors that impact migration	*Climate Change Drives Nomads to Cities*
	Secrets of the Happiest Places on Earth	Compare and contrast yourself with another person	Take a life satisfaction survey **Strategy:** Making general and specific comparisons	*The Secrets of Long Life*
	The Boy with the Amber Necklace: 3,500 years ago, Stonehenge was attracting visitors from all over the world. The question is: Who were they?	Recount a story **Strategy:** Using a graphic organizer to help you tell a story	Explain mysterious places in the world **Strategy:** Refuting a theory	*Discoveries in a Village Near Stonehenge* **Pronunciation:** Differences between American English and British English
	Making Mars the New Earth: What would it take to green the red planet, and should we do it?	Write a counterargument **Strategy:** Making a counterargument	Speak for a minute about space exploration	*Profiles in Exploration*

World Class 2 Student Book Walkthrough

Explore a Unit

The first half of each unit leads students through guided and communicative practice to master target structures.

Stunning images and thought-provoking questions encourage learners to **think critically** about the unit theme.

Clearly stated **Unit Outcomes** provide a roadmap of learning for the student.

Relevant, high frequency vocabulary is practiced in contextualized exercises.

The **Grammar** section allows learners to refine their grammar skills and practice the grammar through first controlled and then open-ended activities.

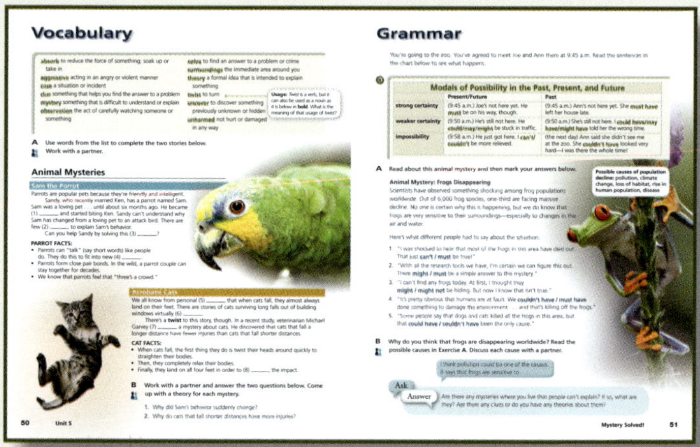

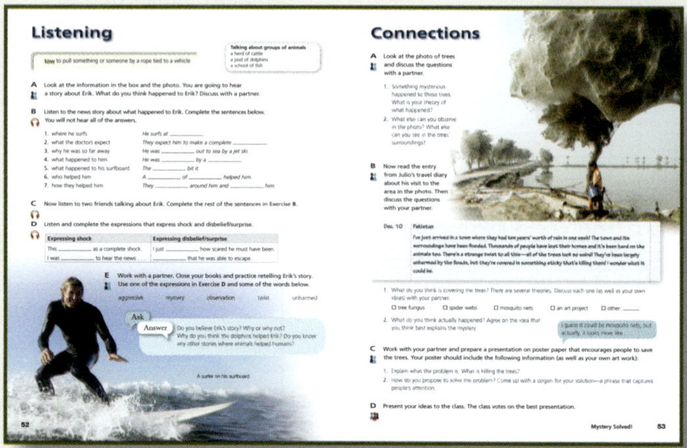

Listening activities encourage learners to listen for and consolidate key information, reinforcing the language, and allowing learners to personalize and think critically about the information they hear.

The **Connections** section allows learners to synthesize the vocabulary and grammar they have learned through personalized communication.

The second half of the unit focuses on skill-building and communication. The strands build on one another with a final communicative task before Expanding Your Fluency. For this reason, the order of strands may vary from unit to unit.

Learners are encouraged to perform **Speaking** tasks in pairs and groups. Where appropriate, **strategies** are provided to ensure students' successful communication.

The **Video** section brings the world into the classroom with authentic clips, including news stories, PSAs, and National Geographic documentaries.

Pronunciation boxes offer support and tips as well as cross reference to full explanation and practice in the appendix.

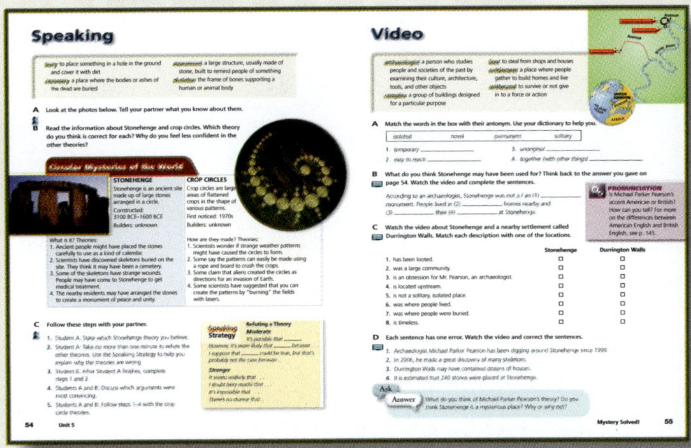

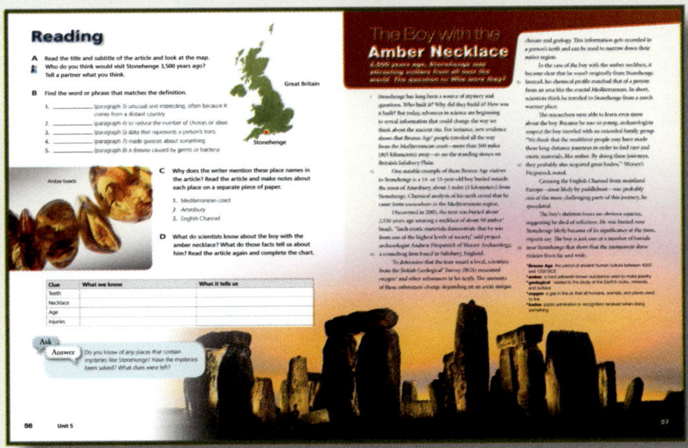

Learners navigate **interesting and relevant readings** from National Geographic through pre-, while-, and post-reading activities, helping them to comprehend the main idea and key details of the passage.

The **Writing** section includes writing models to prompt learners to complete a functional piece of writing and also serves as a culminating activity in many units.

The **Expanding Your Fluency** section allows learners to apply the language they have learned throughout the unit in real-world tasks and offers self-assessment checks.

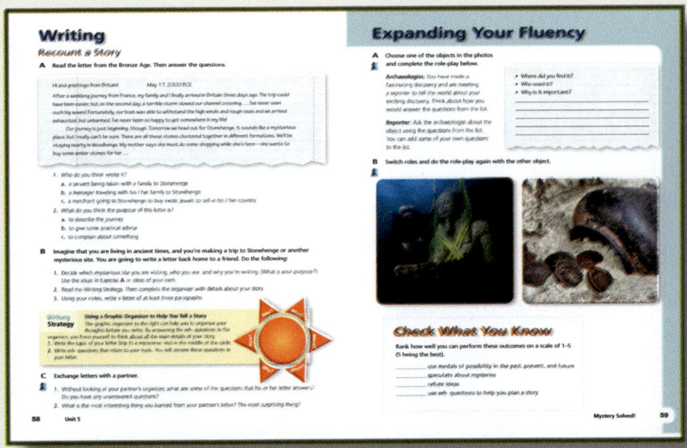

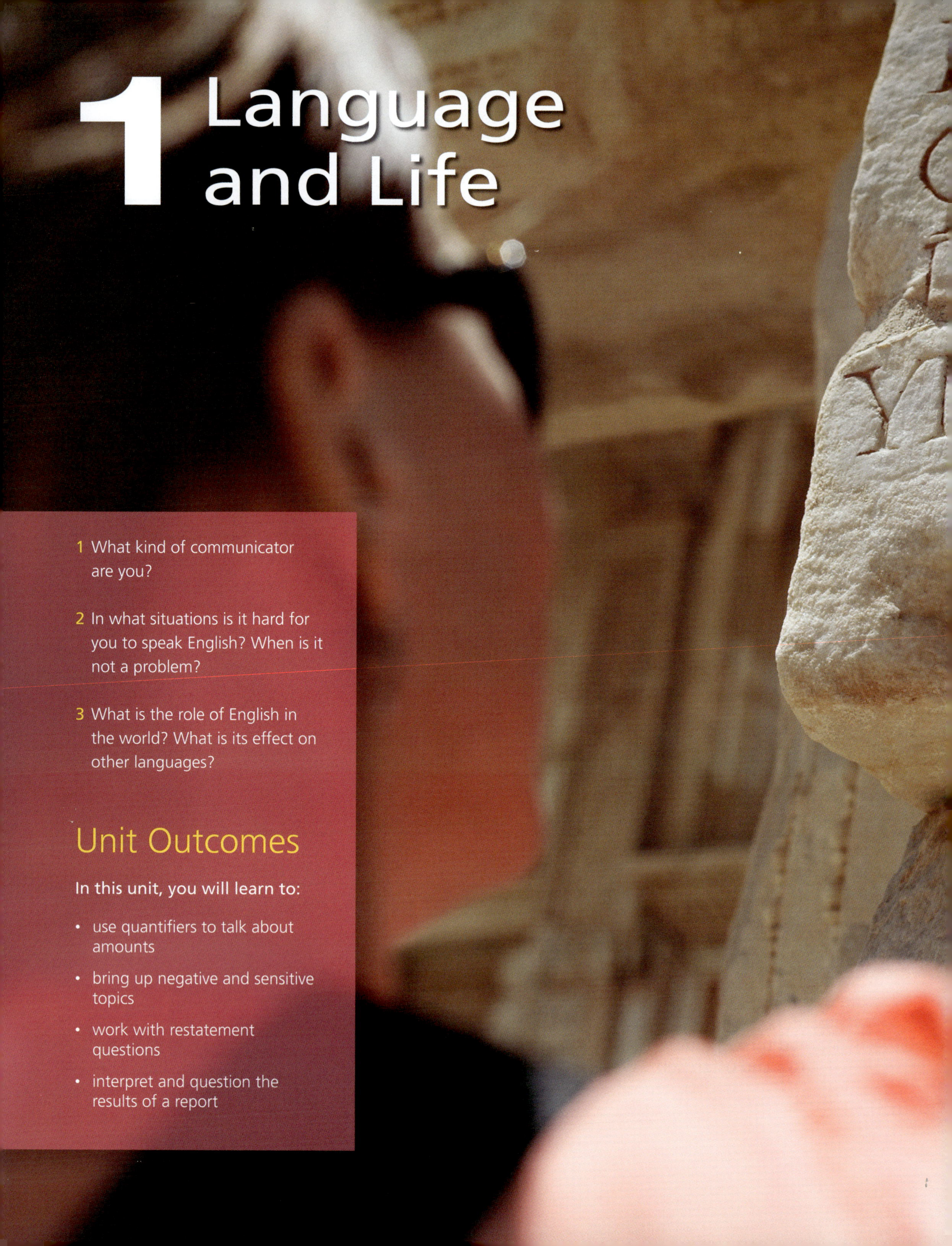

1 Language and Life

1 What kind of communicator are you?

2 In what situations is it hard for you to speak English? When is it not a problem?

3 What is the role of English in the world? What is its effect on other languages?

Unit Outcomes

In this unit, you will learn to:

- use quantifiers to talk about amounts
- bring up negative and sensitive topics
- work with restatement questions
- interpret and question the results of a report

Vocabulary

adapt to change ideas or behavior in order to deal with something successfully
clarify to explain something in order to make it easier to understand
collaborative done by two or more people working together
conflict a serious argument about something important
impulsive doing and saying things suddenly without thinking about it carefully
knowledge information and understanding about a subject
possess to have or to own
remark something that you say (fact or opinion)
sensitive showing an understanding of others' feelings
switch to change
whine to complain in an annoying way about something unimportant

A How do you communicate? Read these questions and think about your answers.

1. Your boss just asked you to lead a very important meeting tomorrow. Do you feel . . .
   a. great? (You love a challenge.) b. nervous? (You'll be awake all night worrying.)
   c. annoyed? (You are a confident communicator, but don't like being asked at the last minute.)
2. Among your friends, you're the one who . . .
   a. remains calm during conflicts. b. helps everyone with sensitive issues.
   c. avoids talking about anything uncomfortable.
3. You're having a bad day. Your friend calls to whine about homework. Do you . . .
   a. listen patiently? b. end the phone call quickly?
   c. switch the topic to your own terrible day?
4. Your idea of a good communicator is someone who . . .
   a. isn't afraid to speak up. b. can adapt to different conversational topics easily.
   c. possesses a lot of knowledge about many topics.
5. At your friend's wedding, someone passes you the microphone suddenly and asks you to make some congratulatory remarks. You haven't prepared anything to say. Do you . . .
   a. smile and try your best? b. pass the microphone on to someone else?
   c. pull another friend in to talk with you?
6. You're having a conversation in English when you don't understand what one person has said. Do you . . .
   a. ask the person to clarify? b. stay silent now and ask for an explanation later?
   c. keep it to yourself and try to figure it out later?

B In pairs, ask each other the questions above. Explain your answers.

C Use two or three of these words to tell your partner what kind of communicator he/she is. Explain why you think so. Does your partner agree?

careful	collaborative	confident	impulsive
nervous	reserved	sensitive	whiney

Grammar

Quantifiers	
General amounts	**Specific amounts (within a group)**
Quantifiers describing general amounts are followed by plural count nouns and noncount nouns.	Quantifiers that describe specific amounts are followed by singular count nouns (except *both* and sometimes *each*).
large amount → **All students** have cell phones.	All members of a group
A lot of students call their parents after school.	**Each/Every student** has a cell phone.
They spend **a lot of time** on their phones.	**Each of** ** the **students** has a cell phone.
There are **many students** studying English.	**Any student** in this class can converse in English.
Quite a few students speak English well.	
Some students need help with their homework.	Talking about two things
I have **some free time** and can help you.	The meeting will be on Monday or Tuesday.
A few* students study other foreign languages.	**Both** days** are fine with me.
We don't have **much time** to study for the exam.	**Either day** is fine.
nothing → **None** of the **students** like homework.	**Neither day** works well for me.
*Another common expression with *few* is *very few* (which is an even smaller amount).	***Each of** and **both** are followed by a plural count noun.

Much is not used alone in affirmative statements. Use *a lot of* instead: ~~*She has much time*~~. *She has a lot of time.*

A Read the survey and choose the best answer for each item.

Communication between Teachers and Parents/Students (Percentages refer to "yes" answers.)			
		Parents	**Students**
Who works full-time in your family?	fathers mothers	98% 92%	
Do you use our school's Web site to get information?		50%	100%
How do you prefer to get information from teachers?	face-to-face e-mail telephone	33% 67% 0%	10% 90% 0%

In (1) **many / much** families, (2) **both / neither** parents have full-time jobs. (3) **Some / All** of the students use their school's Web site for information while only (4) **some / all** of the parents do. (5) **A lot of / Very few** students would like to get information from their teachers face-to-face, but (6) **quite a few / very few** parents would. (7) **Both / Either** parents and students prefer to communicate with the teacher by e-mail. (8) **Neither / Either** prefers to get information by telephone. Parents don't have (9) **much / many** time to meet teachers face-to-face at school. Teachers should communicate with parents through (10) **both / neither** e-mail and face-to-face conversations.

B Ask at least three classmates the questions in the survey. Report your results back to a partner.

Listening

convey to express a thought or feeling so that it is understood

A Read the Listening Strategy. Then listen to three statements from a lecture. What is the meaning of the words below? On a separate piece of paper, write your answers. Look at the Listening Strategy again. Which method does the speaker use to define each word in the lecture?

1. content (of your message)
2. objective
3. straightforward

Listening Strategy

Listening for definitions If you are listening to a lecture or a speech, the speaker will often give cues when they are going to define unfamiliar language. Being familiar with these techniques will help you take advantage of these clarifications.

a. Pausing to give the definition within the sentence: *What is the best way to convey—or express—your message clearly?*
b. Using language to signal a definition: *Another way of saying this is: What is the best way to express your ideas clearly?*
c. Asking the audience directly if they know the word: *Do you know what the word* convey *means? It means "to express."*

B Listen to the first part of the lecture and complete the notes.

You	Create a clear message	Choose the right channel
(1) ______ your objective (why?) Know your (2) ______ (who?) Plan the content (what?)	Use this method (K.I.S.S.): **K** (3) ______ **I**t **S**traightforward and **S** (4) ______	What does the person receiving the message (5) ______? How much (6) ______ do you have? Do you need to (7) ______ and (8) ______ a lot of questions? Is the content (9) ______?

PRONUNCIATION As you listen, notice how the speaker stresses certain words in the lecture. Which words do you notice being stressed? For more on stress with content and function words, see p. 144.

C Listen to the second part of the lecture and match the style of communication (a–d) with the person the speaker uses it with. List key words explaining why she uses that style with each person.

a. cell phone
b. text message
c. landline phone[1]
d. video chat

___ 1. husband reason: ______________
___ 2. son reason: ______________
___ 3. mother reason: ______________
___ 4. friend reason: ______________

Ask Answer Tell your partner one piece of information from the lecture that you found useful. How do you like to communicate with your teacher? Your parents? Your best friend?

[1] traditional or home phone

Connections

A Would you ever get involved in these situations? Discuss with a partner and explain your answers.

1. Ask a teacher how he / she decided your grade.
2. Critique a coworker's work habits with him / her.
3. Complain to a friend about his / her bad habit.

B Follow the steps below. Be sure to use the vocabulary and grammar from this unit.

1. Read through the three role-play situations and make sure you understand them.
2. Study the language in the box.
3. Choose a role-play with a partner. Use the boxed language to get started.
4. After you finish your role-play, pick another situation and switch roles.

Role-play 1: You and your teacher
Your English essay was due last week. You started on the assignment early, did a lot of research, and worked really hard on it. You just got your paper back from your teacher, and you received a poor grade. You're surprised and frustrated. On top of that, your friend completed the same assignment, wrote half as many pages, and spent almost no time on it. He received a good grade. You want an explanation from your teacher.

Role-play 2: You and your coworker
You are working on an important project at work with one other coworker. You have noticed that your coworker takes long work breaks, and when he's at his desk, he spends a lot of time surfing the Net and chatting with friends on the telephone. You're getting worried that you won't be able to meet your deadline if he doesn't start working harder. You need to talk to him and find out what's going on.

Role-play 3: You and a friend
You're getting frustrated. The last time you met to go to the movies, your friend was thirty-five minutes late. Her tardiness is becoming a habit: She's usually at least thirty minutes late whenever you get together. You know that your friend is very busy being a full-time student and working part-time, but you are tired of waiting for her all the time. You want to talk to her about it.

Bringing up a sensitive topic	**Bringing up a negative subject**
Can I talk to you for a minute?	I don't mean to be rude, but . . .
Do you mind if I ask you something?	I'm afraid I have some bad news.
I have to tell you something.	I don't know how to tell you this, but . . .
There's something I need to tell you.	

Ask Answer Which situation do you think would be the hardest to deal with in real life?

Reading

A student in India writes an essay about her school in Punjabi.

distinct noticeably separate or different
linguist a person who specializes in the study of languages
preservation protection (for the future)
vanish to disappear

A Read the title and subtitle and skim the rest of the article on page 7. On a separate piece of paper, write a short answer to the questions. Read the article to check your answers and make any necessary changes.

1. Why do you think so many languages are dying out?
2. What happens when a language dies?

Reading Strategy

Working with restatement questions You will see restatement questions like the ones in Exercise **B** on tests. When choosing the best answer, make sure the restatement . . .
1. does not leave out any essential information.
2. does not change the meaning of the original sentence in any significant way.

B Study the Reading Strategy. Then read each sentence (❶, ❷, ❸) in the article on page 7 and choose the best restatement (a, b, or c) for each sentence. Why are the other choices incorrect? Discuss your answers with a partner.

❶ (line 21)
a. It's truly incredible how rich India's linguistic tradition is.
b. There are many languages in India that we know nothing about.
c. You can study languages at a basic level and not be able to communicate well.

❷ (line 33)
a. Our values and how we live are different from culture to culture.
b. When a culture's language disappears, we lose a view of life that we all share.
c. The main thing that disappears with a language is that culture's distinct view on the human experience.

❸ (line 46)
a. It costs more money to preserve India's culture than it does to protect its languages.
b. People are already preserving some parts of India's culture and they should also protect its languages.
c. In a culture that is as rich as India's, we must continue to preserve buildings and animal life.

C With a partner, find words that have the same or similar meanings.

paragraph 1	in danger ________________
paragraph 2	release ________________
paragraph 5	complicated ________________
paragraph 8	old ________________

Ask Answer What minority languages do you know of? Are there any minority languages in your country? What is their status?

What Happens When **a Language Dies?**

Experts believe that more than half of the world's roughly seven thousand languages will vanish by the end of this century alone, at the rate of one language every two weeks.

India is known for its linguistic and cultural diversity. According to official estimates, the country is home to at least four hundred distinct languages, but many experts believe the actual number is probably around seven hundred. Unfortunately, in a situation that is found in many other countries around the world, many of India's languages are at risk of dying out.

The effects of so many languages disappearing could be a cultural disaster. Each language is like a unique key that can unlock local knowledge and attitudes about medicine, the environment, weather and climate patterns, spiritual beliefs, art, and history.

A group of linguists working on disappearing languages has identified "hotspots" where local languages are at risk of disappearing. These are places with rich linguistic diversity, but high risk of language extinction because there are few remaining speakers. And in these areas, there is often a lack of recordings or texts that would help with language preservation.

❶"India has this incredible wealth of languages, but many have not even been described at a basic level," said David Harrison, a linguistics professor at Swarthmore College in the United States.

All through history, languages have naturally ebbed and flowed,[1] becoming popular before gradually falling from use. But a complex mix of economic, social, and cultural factors[2] is now causing them to disappear at a faster pace. For example, in rural Indian villages, Hindi or English are popular with younger workers because those languages are often required when they travel to larger towns for work.

❷"When a language dies, what is primarily lost is the expression of a unique vision of what it means to be human," said David Crystal, honorary professor of linguistics at the University of Wales in the United Kingdom, and author of the book *Language Death.*

With growing interest in language diversity, it may be possible for disappearing languages to find new life. Awareness of language preservation has grown due to state-funded language programs and new academic centers created for the study of endangered languages. It's also becoming increasingly possible to study minor languages at the college level, thus helping to ensure[3] their survival.

❸"Just as people are doing so much to save the tiger or preserve ancient temples in India, it is as important to protect linguistic diversity, which is a part of India's cultural wealth and a monument to human genius," says David Harrison.

[1] **ebbed and flowed** come and go
[2] **factors** something that affects an event, decision, or situation
[3] **to ensure** to guarantee

Video

detect to find or discover that something is present
document to record the details of an event
endure to continue to exist
slave someone who is the property of another person
threatened endangered

A The title of the video you are going to watch is *A Hidden Language Recorded*. What do you think the video is going to be about? Write your answer on a separate piece of paper. Then watch the video and check your answer.

B Read questions 1–4. Then watch the video again and choose the best answer for each question.

1. Why was it difficult for the team to reach their destination?
   a. They didn't have a special permit.
   b. The area was very remote.
   c. They didn't have enough money.
2. Why is Koro a "surprise" language?
   a. because it was unknown previously
   b. because it contains only about eight hundred words
   c. because it's currently spoken only by people under 20
3. What will happen if Koro speakers switch to another language?
   a. They will have better job opportunities.
   b. Their cultural heritage will disappear.
   c. They will be able to communicate more easily.
4. Why did the expedition record Koro speakers?
   a. They wanted to compare it to the other languages.
   b. They wanted to learn to speak it.
   c. They wanted to document it.

C Summarize what you learned from the video. Make some notes and make sure you cover the points below. Then share your summary with a partner.

1. Country where Koro is spoken
2. Number of Koro speakers
3. Possible origin of the language
4. How researchers discovered it
5. Why they want to record it

Arunachal Pradesh State in India, where Koro is spoken

Ask Answer What do you think of the Enduring Voices Project? Can it really succeed? If so, what is considered a success in this situation?

Writing

Write a Report Summary

A Read the summary of a report about English in Europe. Then discuss the questions below with a partner.

<u>Overview</u>

Worldwide, English is the preferred language of the business elite. However, statistics show that the use of English in business, finance, and technology is moving beyond CEOs and upper-level managers to general workers too. Nowadays, not knowing English can affect hiring and advancement opportunities. In Europe, being able to communicate in English is not an option anymore—it's becoming a requirement.

<u>Relevant Information</u>

- Workers who speak English tend to make more money.
- Very few of those who don't speak English are promoted to managerial positions.
- In the Netherlands and Sweden, all students study English from an early age.
- A majority of Europeans surveyed between the ages of 15 and 24 speak English. The number was much smaller for those 55 and older.
- In another survey, almost half of Europeans said they spoke English. Almost a third said they "spoke it well."

<u>Next Steps</u>

- Some countries are behind others in English education. Countries with fewer English speakers must be given financial assistance to increase educational opportunities there.
- Non-English-speaking employees should be offered either on-site English classes or financial support to take classes on their own.
- In many countries, the very young and the very old have fewer opportunities to study English. Special classes must be developed for these sectors of the population.

1. What is the purpose of the report? Why do you think it was created? By whom?
2. Who might read it? Where might you read a report like this?
3. Did any of the information surprise you? Why or why not?
4. What do you think of the suggested next steps? Do you agree with them? Why or why not?

Did you know?

English is considered by some to be a "killer language." As English is given more attention and importance in countries worldwide, speakers of English can "crowd out" or "kill off" the culture and languages of people who speak other languages. In Europe, many minority languages enjoy popularity and government protection, but that is certainly not the case for minority languages internationally.

B Think about the status of English education in your country. Complete the survey with a partner. If you live in a country with minority languages, you may also want to reflect on the status of English versus those languages.

English facts about ____________________ (country name)

1. **Most / Some / Very few** businesses require employees to speak some English.

   Industries that use English most: ____________________

2. **Most / Some / Very few** employees who speak English make more money.
3. **All / Some / Very few** children begin studying English in primary school.
4. **All / Some / Very few** people 55 and older speak English.
5. Overall, **all / some / very few** people speak basic English (greetings and simple sentences).

Based on these findings, we would suggest the following:

1. ______________________________
2. ______________________________
3. ______________________________

C Read the Writing Strategy. Then use the information in Exercise **B** to write a report summary together. Use Exercise **A** as a model.

D Join another pair. Read their report summary and answer questions 1–3 in the Writing Checklist.

Writing Checklist

Does the report summary . . .

1. have a brief, clear Overview?
2. use Relevant Information that's easy to understand?
3. give you a clear idea of the Next Steps?

Writing Strategy

Writing a Report Summary

1. Your Overview should give some background and clearly explain the purpose of the report.
2. Choose Relevant Information that best explains the situation simply and clearly. Imagine that someone who has never been to your country is reading this report.
3. For each recommendation in the Next Steps, state the problem in the first sentence. In the second sentence, write your recommendation.

Speaking

A You are going to present your report summary. Decide who will present what. Practice giving your report with a partner.

Speaking Strategy

Interpreting the Results (for the speakers)

The way I see it . . .
As far as I'm concerned . . .
I strongly believe that . . .
Without a doubt, . . .

Questioning the Results (for the listeners)

While ___ may be true, it's also important to remember that . . .
I see your point, but one problem with what you're saying is . . .

B Join another pair and give your report.

1. **Speakers:** Present the report. Interpret what we can learn from the statistics you found. Remember to speak clearly and look at your audience.
2. **Listeners:** After the presentation, if there is anything you disagreed with, speak up.

TIP Practice "reading and looking up." Read a phrase or sentence from your report silently before you speak. Then look up from the text at your audience and say it aloud. This will help you to maintain a connection with your audience.

Expanding Your Fluency

Loanwords in English are words that are taken from another language, sometimes with a change in meaning. An example of a loanword from Spanish to English is *aficionado*, which means "fan" in both languages.

A Read through the questions with a partner. Make sure you understand them.

1. This word, which describes **a yellow-skinned fruit loved by monkeys**, came to English from Africa through Spanish or Portuguese. What is the English word?
2. The **samovar** is a metal container used to heat water for tea. Samovars became widely popular in the city of St. Petersburg in the nineteenth century. What country is the word **samovar** from?
3. This word refers to **a permanent mark or design made on the skin with ink.** In the Tahitian language, you say "tatu." What is the word in English?
4. In Swedish, the word "isberg" means "ice mountain." In English, the loanword means **"a huge piece of ice floating in the ocean."** What is the word in English?
5. This popular morning beverage comes from the Arabic word "qahwah" and **it may be named after the Kaffa region** in Ethiopia. What is the word for this drink in English?
6. You might want some of this **red sauce** (from the Chinese word "koechiap") the next time you have a hamburger. What is the word in English?
7. The word "broccoli" in English comes from **a European country that is known for its appreciation of good food and wine.** What is the name of that country?
8. In Persian, the word "paejamah" can be divided into "pae" (leg) and "jamah" (clothing). In English, the word refers to **something you would put on before bedtime.** What is the word in English?

B Join another pair. Take turns asking each other the questions. Score one point for each correct answer.

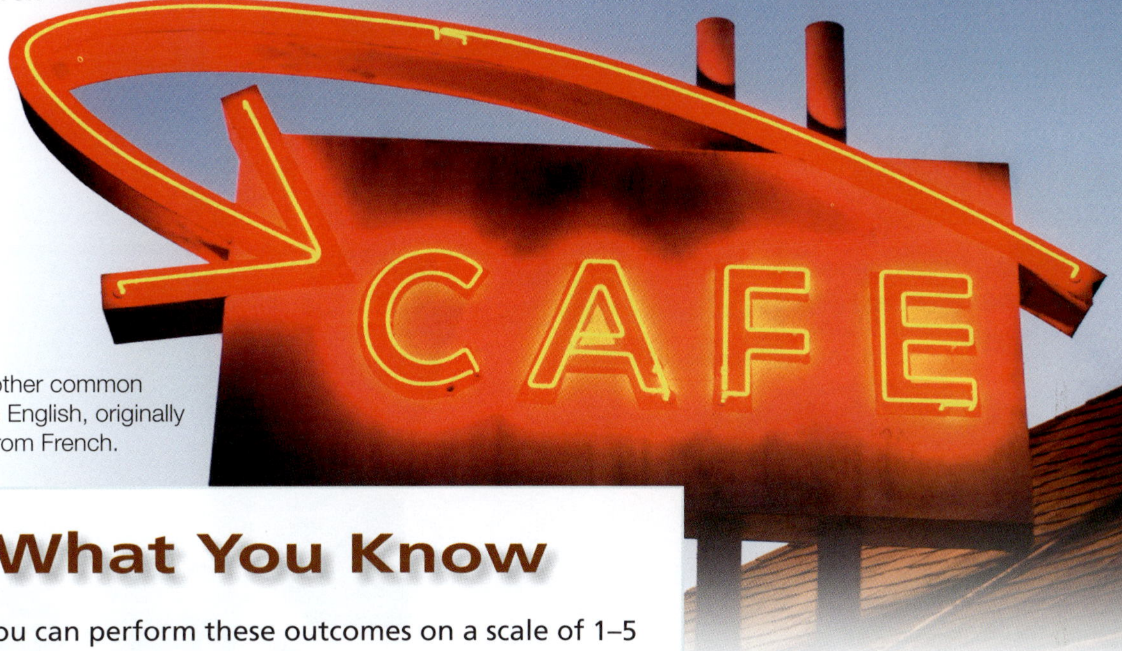

Cafe is another common loanword in English, originally borrowed from French.

Check What You Know

Rank how well you can perform these outcomes on a scale of 1–5 (5 being the best).

__________ use quantifiers to talk about amounts
__________ bring up negative and sensitive topics
__________ work with restatement questions
__________ interpret and question the results of a report

2 Money Talks

1 Read the title of the unit. If money could talk, what do you think it would say?

2 Look at the photo. Where do you think this place is? What do you think the people are doing? What is the bowl on the ground for?

3 In general, would you say that you are good or bad with money? Explain.

Unit Outcomes

In this unit, you will learn to:

- describe spending habits and preferences
- use noun clauses to explain thoughts in more detail
- determine the meaning of unfamiliar words in a text
- consider the advantages and disadvantages of something

TISAK media
najveći iz

Vocabulary

affluent wealthy
budget a plan that shows the amount of money available to spend
credit a method that allows you to buy things and pay for them later
debt money that you owe
disposable income the money remaining after your bills are paid
loan money you borrow or lend
materialistic valuing money and possessions very highly
pay back to return money that you owe someone
sacrifice to give up something valuable to help yourself or others
save up (for something) to put aside money for future use
splurge to spend a lot of money on something, usually something you don't need
thrifty careful with money
value to attach importance to something

Word Partnership

What do these expressions that use *credit* mean?
~ card, ~ history, live on ~, good/bad ~

A Read the two profiles. Try to guess which word from the word bank completes each sentence. Then listen and write the correct form of the word.

Lukas

My parents took loans and went into (1) _______ to buy a house and lots of expensive things. They lived on credit, and today they're still (2) _______ the money they owe. I, on the other hand, have always stayed within a budget. I rent a small but comfortable apartment, ride my bike places, and spend less overall. I guess we just (3) _______ different things.

Carla

My parents worked hard and saved up to send me to a good university. They (4) _______ a lot for me and always worried about money. Today, I'm a successful businesswoman with a disposable income that my parents never had. I've got a beautiful home, take regular vacations, and (5) _______ on nice things for myself once in a while—and why shouldn't I?

B Discuss the questions with a partner.

1. Which words from the word bank describe Lukas and Carla? How about their parents? Why?
2. How have things changed for each of these people in one generation?
3. Can you relate to any of these people's experiences? Explain with an example.

C Think of two more questions. Each should use a different item from the word bank. Then take turns asking and answering the questions with a partner.

1. What's something you're saving up for?
2. Are you a thrifty person?
3. ____________________________________?
4. ____________________________________?

Grammar

Noun Clauses	
noun clauses starting with *that*	I like this jacket. How much is it? I think **(that) it is $50**.
noun clauses starting with a *wh-* word	I like this jacket. How much is it? I don't know **how much it is**.

Some **noun clauses** begin with the word *that*.
Other **noun clauses** begin with a *wh-* word (*who, what, where, why, how, when, which, whose*). These clauses follow statement word order even though they start with a question word.

Certain verbs are commonly followed by a noun clause . . .
- verbs that describe an opinion, feeling, or mental state: *assume, believe, guess, forget, hope, know, remember, suppose, think, understand, wonder*
- verbs that describe something someone said: *admit, explain, mention, say, tell*

A Choose the correct answer for each sentence. Then check answers and practice the dialog with a partner.

A: Joe eats out every day. I wonder how (1) **can he / he can** afford it.
B: He (2) **told me / told to me that** he just got a new job.
A: Do you know (3) **where is he / where he is** working?
B: I think (4) **that is at / he works at** a cafe near school.

B Change the question to a noun clause that starts with a *wh-* word.

1. I've just inherited some money. What should I do with it?
   I don't know what I should do with it.
2. Nadia's brother is jealous because she earns more money than he does. Why does he feel that way?
   I wonder ________________.
3. Some people love to shop. Why do they like it?
   I don't get ________________.
4. I need to get some money. Where's the closest ATM?
   Do you know ________________?
5. I owe a lot on my credit card. How can I pay the money back fast?
   Can you suggest ________________?
6. I missed class yesterday. What did we do?
   Do you remember ________________?

C With a partner, create short dialogs using the situations in Exercise **B**. In each dialog try to use at least one noun clause starting with *that*.

I've just inherited some money, but I don't know what I should do with it.

I guess that you could splurge on something like a vacation or a new car, but it's probably best to save the money.

Listening

A Look at the photos and then discuss the questions with a partner.

1. How much money do people typically spend on a wedding in your country?
2. Is it worth spending a lot of money on a big TV? Explain your answer.

B You are going to hear two short dialogs. Listen and check the answers that are true about the people. List any key words that helped you make your choices. Then check answers with a partner.

Josh and Tina . . .	**True**	**Key words**
1. are planning to get married this year.	☐	____________
2. want to have a large wedding.	☐	____________
3. come from affluent families.	☐	____________

Marta . . .	**True**	**Key words**
1. has enough money to buy the big TV.	☐	____________
2. has a budget for how much she can spend on a TV.	☐	____________
3. decides to splurge and get the big TV.	☐	____________

C Play the dialogs again and listen for the words in italics. Then choose the correct answers.

1. *cost a fortune* = Something costs **a lot / very little**.
2. *out of my price range* = Something is **really affordable / too expensive**.
3. *maxed out* = The credit card will have **enough / no** credit left.
4. *a steal* = Something is really **cheap / expensive**.

D Discuss the questions with a partner.

1. In Dialog 1, how does the man feel about Josh and Tina's decision? Why? Would you want a wedding like theirs? Why or why not?
2. In Dialog 2, do you think Marta made the right decision? Why or why not? What is something that is out of your price range that you wish you could buy? Why do you want it?

Connections

A Get into a group of three people and do the following:

1. Read the questions. Then together write two more questions of your own. Each question should be related to the topic of money.

   Would you be willing to . . .

   a. loan money to a good friend who might not be able to pay you back?
   b. marry someone who was poor or in debt?
   c. give up your seat on an airplane for cash (and take a different flight the next day)?
   d. use a credit card to splurge on something really expensive?
   e. ____?
   f. ____?

2. On your own, think about your answers to each question.
3. Take six small pieces of paper. Write the letters *a* to *f* on each. Shuffle the papers and place them face down in a pile.
4. One person starts. Turn over a paper and answer that question. (You should not answer the same question twice.) Use one of the expressions in the strategy box to get started. Then explain your answer. Try to speak for at least one minute. Your group members should each ask you one question.
5. When you are done, return the paper to the bottom of the pile. Then it is the next person's turn.
6. Play until everyone has answered all of the questions.

Speaking Strategy

Expressing an Opinion
Yeah, definitely because . . .
I think so . . .
I guess/suppose so, but . . .
I don't know what I'd do, but I guess . . .
I don't think so . . ./I doubt it.
No way./Definitely not.

Notice! Some noun clauses can be shortened using *so*.
Would you loan money to a friend?
I (don't) think so. = I (don't) think that I'd loan money to him.

Reading

A Complete sentences 1 and 2 with words from the box and check answers with a partner. Then look at the photo. This person needs to borrow money to pay for university. Do you think a bank will lend her money? Why or why not?

collateral	interest	lend	qualify

1. To ________ for a bank loan, you must have good credit and even some ________ (extra money, a house or car that you already own). If you don't have these things, a bank won't ________ you the money.
2. When you borrow money from a bank, you have to pay a fee called ________ on the money you borrowed.

Age: 21
Occupation: Part-time cashier in store
Credit history: $300 in the bank, one credit card with $600 on it, doesn't own a car or any property

B Read the strategy box and then the entire article on the next page. When you are done, write a simple definition or synonym for the five boldfaced words on a separate piece of paper. Try to work out the meaning on your own. Then check answers with a partner.

Reading Strategy

Determine the Meaning of Unfamiliar Words in a Text

1. Sometimes it is possible to understand the meaning of unfamiliar words in a reading by analyzing the word's parts: *il* (meaning *not*) + *legible* (meaning *readable*) = difficult to read.
2. You can also use surrounding words to help you: *It's a new type of banking called micro-credit, which gives small loans to poor people.*

C Re-read paragraphs 1 and 2 and then answer the questions on a separate piece of paper.

1. What is micro-credit banking?
2. How is micro-credit banking different from traditional bank loans? List two examples.
3. What is the relationship of each of these numbers to Muhammad Yunus and micro-credit banking?

1976 $5.7 billion 96% a few hundred US dollars 98%

D How does Kiva work? Complete steps 1–7 and then explain the process to a partner.

1. A person who wants to borrow money visits ________________.
2. The person is interviewed to make sure ________________.
3. The borrower's profile is then ________________.
4. People around the world can then read that profile, ________________, and ________________.
5. The borrower uses the money to ________________.
6. The borrower then has a certain amount of time to ________________.
7. Finally, the money is ________________ the lender's account.

Ask Answer Do you think that micro-lending has been successful? Explain with specific examples from the article.

Muhammad Yunus

MICRO LOANS, MACRO IMPACT

They call Muhammad Yunus the "banker of the poor." The economist[1] from Bangladesh and his Grameen Bank **pioneered** a new type of banking known as micro-credit. This type of banking gives small loans to poor people who have no collateral and who do not qualify for traditional bank loans. The program, which Yunus founded in 1976, has enabled millions of Bangladeshis to buy everything from cows to cell phones in order to start and run their own businesses. Since then, Grameen Bank has made an estimated $5.7 billion in loans to more than six million people in Bangladesh, 96% of them women.

Anyone can qualify for the loans, which average a few hundred US dollars. No collateral or credit history is necessary, nor is completing a lot of paperwork (as many of those applying for the loans are **illiterate**). A borrower can only apply for future loans after repaying some of his or her current debts, and to date, the system has a repayment rate of 98%, the bank says. "A hundred dollars may be all a poor person needs to get out of poverty," says Alex Counts, who worked with Yunus in Bangladesh for six years. "You give them a fair deal[2] . . . and they're able to put their motivation and skills to work."

Today, micro-credit projects like Yunus' are helping many around the world. One is an Internet-based lending company called Kiva. It was started in 2005 by two Stanford University graduates who attended a talk given by Muhammad Yunus. Kiva works by connecting regular people who have some extra money to lend with entrepreneurs[3] who need it.

How does the process work? A person who wants to borrow money first visits one of Kiva's "field partners." (These are micro-lending institutions in countries all over the world.) The person is interviewed to make sure that he or she is **legitimate** and will be using the loan in a legal way. Then the person's profile is posted on the Kiva Web site. People around the world can read that profile, open an account on the Kiva site, and make a loan. The person who borrowed the money might use it to start a business, attend school, open a clinic, or build housing. The borrower then has a certain amount of time to repay the money, which is eventually **deposited** back into the lender's account. Lenders receive no interest, though most field partners working with Kiva charge the borrower a fee. Some fees are as little as 8% of the original loan, while others are higher. According to Kiva, more than 700,000 people have received loans, and over 98% of those people have paid back the money.

Yunus, who won the Nobel Peace Prize for his work, believes that offering people micro-loans not only helps them to get out of poverty; it also promotes peace and stability.[4] Sam Daley-Harris, who worked with Yunus, agrees. Achieving peace is about more than stopping war, he says. "A key part of **preventing** conflict is enabling people . . . to care for themselves and their children." This is what micro-credit programs like Grameen Bank and Kiva are helping people to do.

> "A hundred dollars may be all a poor person needs to get out of poverty."

[1] **economist** a person who studies the way in which money is used in society
[2] **fair deal** a good business arrangement
[3] **entrepreneur** a person who starts his or her own business
[4] **stability** a situation that is calm and not likely to change suddenly

Video

headache a big problem
impact to have an effect on someone or something
run out (of something) to have no more of something
snowball to increase rapidly
terms the parts of the contract that all sides must agree on (e.g., how much a loan is for, how long one has to pay it back, etc.)

A Think about what you've already learned from the article about borrowing and lending money. Then discuss the questions with a partner.

1. Why would a person borrow money from a bank?
2. What are some of the benefits of being able to borrow money from a bank? What are some of the risks?

B Watch segment 1 of the video. Then choose the best answer to complete the sentences.

1. You might watch this video to learn . . . .
   a. which banks are the best to borrow from
   b. about the history of banking in the United States
   c. how borrowing money from a bank works
2. The *interest rate* on a loan is . . . .
   a. a fine you pay for not repaying the bank
   b. the money you borrow from the bank
   c. a fee you pay for borrowing money

C Rachel is a musician who needs to borrow some money. Read the outline. Then watch segment 2 of the video and complete the outline.

A. Reason she needs to borrow money: ______________________________
   How much she needs: $____________
B. First loan terms:
   - ____________% APR (annual percentage rate)
   - Must pay back the loan in ____________ year(s)
   - Payment amount per month: $____________
   - If she accepted this loan, she would ____________ of money in ____________ months.
C. She finally finds a loan with a __________ APR and a ____________ time frame.

D Before accepting her loan, what two important things did Rachel learn? Watch segment 3 and choose your answers. Then tell a partner why knowing those two things is important.

☐ the importance of making payments on time
☐ some banks don't lend money to students
☐ how to budget your money
☐ interest rates can change

E Discuss the questions with a partner.

1. Why was Rachel able to pay back her loan on time?
2. In recent years, some banks have allowed people to take loans that were difficult—sometimes even impossible—to pay back. Why would a bank do this? Why is doing this a problem for both the borrower and the bank?

Speaking

profit money that is earned in business minus expenses

A Get into a group of six people: three will be borrowers (entrepreneurs); the other three will be lenders (investors).

ENTREPRENEURS: You need a large amount of money to do something important. On your own . . .

1. Select a reason or think of your own idea.
   - To start a business or invent a product
   - To record an album or film a movie
   - To open a school
   - To build housing
   - Your idea: ________________
2. Answer the questions on a separate piece of paper. You can invent information or use real facts. You have to impress the investors, so be creative.
   - What do you plan to do with the money?
   - Why do you think your idea will be a big success and make you and the investors a lot of money?
   - How much money do you need to get started?

INVESTORS: You're all billionaire investors looking for "the next big thing." You give money to entrepreneurs with great ideas in return for a percentage of the profits they eventually earn.

You're going to interview three entrepreneurs. Each one thinks he/she has a great idea, but they all need a large amount of money to get started. You only want to invest in ideas that are likely to make you money.

Read the three questions in the entrepreneurs' section and together think of others you could ask.

Grand opening

B Each investor should pair up with an entrepreneur. The investor should use his or her questions to interview the entrepreneur and take notes on the person's replies. Repeat this step until each investor has interviewed each entrepreneur. You will have three minutes per interview.

C When the interviews are over, do the following:

- **Investors:** On your own, review your notes. Of the three entrepreneurs you interviewed, who do you want to invest in—all of them, one of them, or none of them? Why?
- **Entrepreneurs:** Get together in a group of three. Explain to the other entrepreneurs what you need money to do. Do you think you're going to get it? Why or why not?

D Get back together in your original group from Exercise **A**. Each investor should take turns explaining their investment decision to the group. Were the investors' choices the same? Which entrepreneur's idea was the most popular?

E Change roles and repeat Exercises **A** through **D**.

Writing

Write about Advantages and Disadvantages

A What are some of the advantages and disadvantages of using a credit card? With a partner, list as many ideas as you can on a separate piece of paper. Then compare ideas with the class.

B Read the paragraphs and then answer the questions below.

> Using a credit card has advantages and disadvantages. **One obvious advantage is that** you can buy anything you want or need immediately, even if it is expensive. Let's say, for example, that you really need a new laptop, but you don't have the money for it. Instead of waiting and saving up for it, you could use your credit card to buy the computer and pay for it a little at a time. **Another benefit of using a credit card is that** you can earn points on some cards to buy things. Each time you buy something with your card, you get points. Later you can use these to get other things for free.
>
> There are disadvantages of using credits cards, though. **One disadvantage is that** a credit card makes it too easy to buy things. If you go into a store and have $50, for example, you can only spend that much money. But with a credit card, you can buy many more things, including things you can't afford. This can cause you to go into debt. **Another drawback is that** . . .

Start the essay with a clear topic sentence that tells your readers what the text is about.

Use the boldfaced phrases to introduce and transition from one idea to the next.

1. What two advantages does the writer mention in the first paragraph?
2. The writer explains each advantage with an example. Underline each example in the paragraph.
3. What is another disadvantage of having a credit card? Finish the second paragraph with your own idea. Remember to include an example to explain your point. Then compare ideas with a partner.

C Complete steps 1 and 2 below.

1. Many students today must get a loan to attend university. What are the advantages and disadvantages of taking a large loan to attend university? Outline two advantages and two disadvantages on a separate piece of paper. Think of an example to support each one.
2. Use your outline to write a two-paragraph essay. Remember to start off with a clear topic sentence, explain each advantage and disadvantage with a detailed example, and use the boldfaced phrases from Exercise **B** to transition from one idea to the next.

D Exchange papers with a partner. Read your partner's essay and use the checklist to make sure the essay is complete.

Writing Checklist

The essay . . .

- has a clear topic sentence.
- identifies two advantages and two disadvantages and explains each with a detailed example.
- uses the boldfaced phrases in Exercise **B** to introduce and transition from one idea to the next.

Expanding Your Fluency

Read the six situations (a–f) below. Then do steps 1–3 with a partner.

1. Write a simple definition for each underlined word or phrase.
2. Identify if each underlined word or phrase is related to saving or spending money.
3. Use at least one of the underlined words or phrases and other vocabulary you learned in this unit to write a short dialog. Then perform your dialog for another pair.

a. I've got a nest egg of $100,000 in my bank account that I can use as a down payment on a condo.
b. Lunch is my treat today. You paid for it the last time we went out together.
c. Martin is more than thrifty; he's a total cheapskate. He never spends money on *anything*.
d. We know the restaurant's owner so our meals were on the house. We didn't pay for anything.
e. It's hard to make ends meet every month when you don't make a lot of money.
f. I'm broke. Could you lend me $50 until payday? I promise I'll pay you back.

Check What You Know

Rank how well you can perform these outcomes on a scale of 1–5 (5 being the best).

_________ describe spending habits and preferences
_________ use noun clauses to explain thoughts in more detail
_________ determine the meaning of unfamiliar words in a text
_________ consider the advantages and disadvantages of something

3 Bright Lights, Big Cities

1 What are some of the challenges of living in a big city?

2 What factors make a city a nice place to live?

3 How does the movement of people affect life in the city? Life in the countryside?

Unit Outcomes

In this unit, you will learn to:

- express actions and conditions in the passive voice
- use an outline to summarize
- use statistics to understand a writer's point of view
- write a summary

Vocabulary

chaotic in a state of complete disorder
community a group of people that live in a particular place
cosmopolitan full of people from many different countries
descendants people of later generations
district an area of a town or country
dynamic full of energy
global affecting all parts of the world; international
immigrant a person who moves permanently to a different country
inhabitant a person who lives in a particular place
livable suitable for living in
manageable able to be dealt with easily
metropolitan relating to a large, busy city

Word Partnership

How many words with *mega-* (= extremely large) and *multi-* (= large number) can you locate below? What do they mean?

A Read these descriptions of different international destinations. Match each description with the city it describes. (One city is not used.)

a. Cairo, Egypt
b. Moscow, Russia
c. New York, USA
d. São Paulo, Brazil
e. Sydney, Australia

CITIES OF THE WORLD QUIZ

___ 1. This multiethnic city has major communities composed of the descendants of European, Asian, and African immigrants. In fact, the world's largest Japanese population outside of Japan lives in the Liberdade neighborhood in this city. **Fun thing to do:** Join in the Carnival fun.

___ 2. In the 1930s, this city's population was over ten million, making it the world's first "megacity." A third of the inhabitants of this multicultural city come from other countries and it is the home to many multinational corporations. **Fun thing to do:** Take the ferry to the Statue of Liberty.

___ 3. Home to approximately seventeen million people in its metropolitan area, this megapolis is known as the "Mother of the World." This dynamic and chaotic city is a great home base for sightseeing trips. **Fun thing to do:** Visit the oldest district in the city and see walls from Roman times.

___ 4. Small enough to be manageable, yet large enough to maintain a cosmopolitan atmosphere, this global city of sea and surf is often rated as one of the most livable cities in the world. **Fun thing to do:** Go sailing under the Harbour Bridge or take a jog along the cliffs.

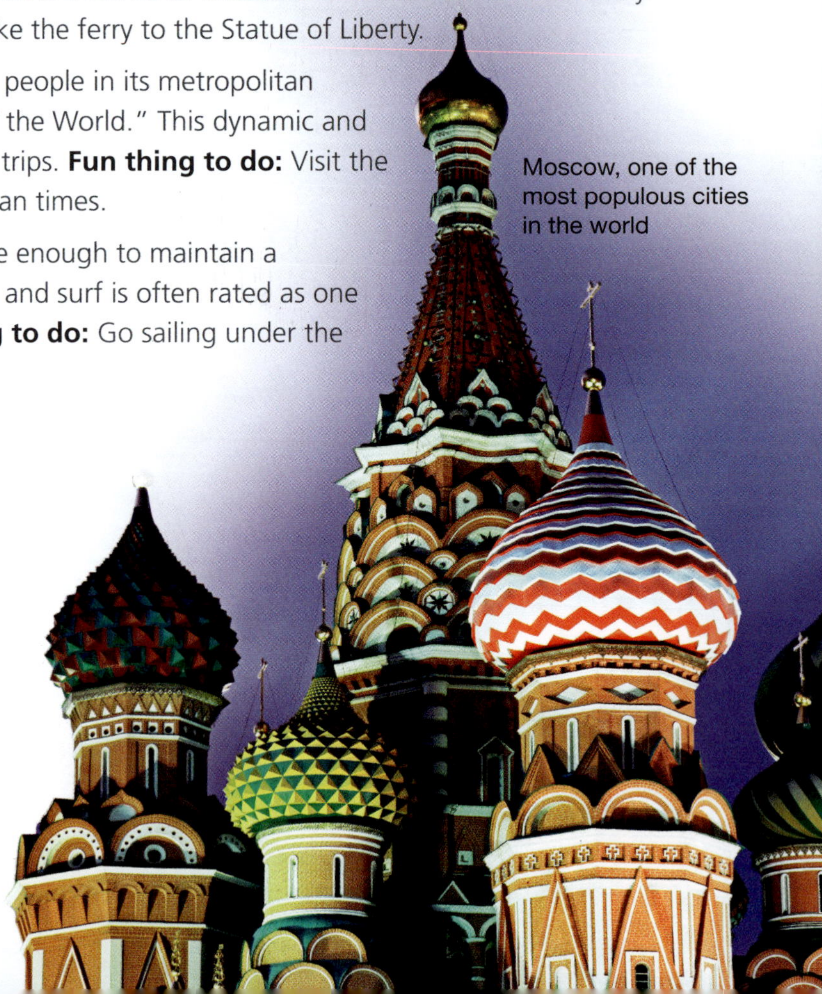

Moscow, one of the most populous cities in the world

B Answer the questions with a partner.

1. How many inhabitants are there in the metropolitan area nearest you?
2. Which adjective(s) would you use to describe this metropolitan area?
3. Does your area have many immigrants? Where are they from?
4. Is there a lot of construction and growth going on where you live?
5. What's the most interesting district where you live? Why?

Grammar

Notice! The form for the dynamic and stative passive is the same: a form of *be* + the past participle.

Dynamic and Stative Passive	
Dynamic Passive Belize City, the former capital, **was** nearly **destroyed** by a hurricane in 1961. The government **was moved** to Belmopan in 1970.	**Stative Passive** Belmopan, the new capital, **is situated** inland on safer ground, but Belize City **is** still **known** as the financial and cultural center of the country.
• This form of the passive expresses an action. The focus is on the receiver of the action, not the performer. • Use *by* + agent to name the performer of the action. (We don't use a *by* phrase when the performer is unimportant, unknown, or is obvious.) • The past participle functions more like a verb than an adjective. It expresses the action.	• This form of the passive describes a state or condition. • Because there is no action being expressed, it's impossible to name the agent. • Instead, we use a form of the passive followed by a preposition (not necessarily *by*). • The past participle functions more like an adjective than a verb. It describes the subject.
Verbs used with dynamic passive: *built, created, destroyed, divided, moved, sent*	***Verbs used with stative passive:*** *acquaint (with), associate (with), cover (with), crowd (with), dress (in), involve (with), know (as), made (of), situate (on)*

A Read about the Nebuta Festival. Complete the description with the passive forms of the verbs in parentheses. Add a preposition when necessary. Which passive forms are stative and which are dynamic?

A FUN THING TO DO IN MY CITY

You may not __________ (1. acquaint) the Nebuta Festival. It __________ (2. organize) the city of Aomori, in northern Japan. The main part of the festival is a nighttime parade. Special colorful floats __________ (3. prepare) people in the community. The frames of these floats __________ (4. make) wood and __________ (5. cover) beautiful paper. The inside of each float __________ (6. illuminate) special lights that make them glow. Then the brightly lit floats __________ (7. carry) city residents through the streets. The streets __________ (8. crowd) spectators as well as festival dancers, who __________ (9. dress) special costumes. The dancers __________ (10. accompany) loud drumming music, and the dancers chant noisily as they move through the streets. If you want to __________ (11. involve) the festival, even as a tourist, you can! You just have to rent a costume to dance! The festival __________ (12. associate) an old legend. It is said that many centuries ago, the colorful floats __________ (13. use) soldiers in battle. The soldiers hid inside them in order to trick their enemies.

B Work with a partner. Think of a major event in a city that you know. Use these questions to make some notes about it, but don't write the name of the event down.

- Is the event well known around the world?
- When and where is the event held?
- Why is it celebrated? Is it associated with a particular person or historical event?
- Will you see people dressed in special clothes?
- Are any special foods prepared on that day?
- When will it be celebrated next?

C Present the notes about your event to another pair without naming it. Can they guess what it is?

Listening

rapid fast
renewal the act of restoring

Word Partnership
urban ~renewal, ~planning, ~community, ~development, ~sprawl

A Frank and Jane are talking about the city of Curitiba, Brazil. Listen to the first part of their conversation. Then choose the best answer to complete each sentence.

1. Frank is going to Curitiba for **business / pleasure / school**.
2. Jane visited Curitiba for **business / pleasure / school**.

B Now listen to Frank and Jane's entire conversation. Which one of these topics was *not* mentioned?

a famous person
sightseeing tips
weather conditions
cheap flights
transportation system

C Read the outline. Use the topics in Exercise **B** to complete the information. Then listen and complete the rest of the outline.

Curitiba, Brazil

I. ____________________
   A. best in Brazil
      1. makes the city very __________
   B. constructed in the __________
      1. went from 25,000 to __________ riders a day
II. ____________________: Jaime Lerner
   A. the __________ for many years
      1. associated with positive changes
      2. devoted to creating a __________ city
      3. reduced city's dependence on __________
      4. supported new __________ transit line
III. ____________________
   A. the __________ Line comes every 30 minutes
      1. visits major parks and attractions
   B. see __________ influence in architecture, customs, and food
IV. ____________________
   A. bring a __________ for the cool __________ at night

The Oscar Niemeyer Museum in Curitiba, Brazil

D Using your outline in Exercise **C,** summarize for your partner what Curitiba is known for. What is your city known for? Tell your partner two or three ideas.

Connections

ban to refuse to allow

A Read the statement and discuss with a partner. Do you agree or disagree with it? What kind of small changes could make your city more livable?

Every city can be improved in less than three years by making a series of small changes.

B Talal's city celebrated World Carfree Day (September 22) for the first time this past year. What did they do? Was it a success? Discuss with a partner.

The setup	• All private cars were banned from the city's central district from 9:00 a.m. to 1:00 p.m. (Wednesday). • Signs throughout the metropolitan area informed drivers of road closures. • Traffic police and guards stood at intersections to guide traffic. • Two hundred volunteers set up information booths.
The results	• Some drivers ignored the signs and tried to drive into the city center. • There were a couple traffic jams right outside the city center, but in other areas of the city there were fewer traffic jams. • Citywide, traffic accidents decreased dramatically. • Only one in ten private-car owners left their car at home for the entire day. Most inhabitants drove as usual, simply avoiding the city center.

C Now work with a partner to plan a World Carfree Day where you live. Read the rules and complete the details. Then discuss the questions together.

RULES:

1. World Carfree Day events should be between four and twelve hours long.
2. The carfree area should be at least 5 square kilometers.

DETAILS:

1. The ___________ (name of area) area / district is located in ______________________________ (city).
2. We will be closing this area / district to _________________ (type of transportation) from ________ (start time) to ________ (end time) on ______________ (day of the week).

- Some people are not acquainted with World Carfree Day. How do you plan to advertise it?
- The streets just outside the carfree zone will be filled with vehicles. What will you do to handle that situation?
- How will your plans be coordinated with the public transportation system (buses, trains, etc.) where you live?
- How will you prepare drivers for road closures and any other inconveniences?

D Share your idea for World Carfree Day with another pair of students.

Reading

infrastructure the basic facilities (such as transportation, power supplies, and buildings) that allow a city or organization to function
per capita (the amount) per person
transformation a complete change in the appearance of something (usually for the better)
urbanization the process by which more and more people move from rural areas to the cities

A Skim the article on page 31. What is it about? Complete the sentence.

The article is about the _____ rapid urbanization in Seoul, South Korea.

a. history of   b. pros and cons of   c. author's experience of   d. failure of

Reading Strategy

Locating and Reading Statistics Locate and read the statistical information (as well as the sentences around it) in an article. Paying attention to the kinds of statistics that the author has chosen to present may tell you about his/her overall point of view (positive, negative, or neutral).

B Read the article and match the numbers to what they describe. Then choose the best answer about the author's point of view.

___ 1. paragraph 1: *fewer than three million to ten million*
___ 2. paragraph 1: *less than one hundred*
___ 3. paragraph 2: *1394*
___ 4. paragraph 3: *more than a million*
___ 5. paragraph 5: *half the people*
___ 6. paragraph 6: *twenty-four million*
___ 7. paragraph 6: *28% to 83%*
___ 8. paragraph 6: *fifty-one years to seventy-nine years*

a. people arriving in Seoul after the wars
b. change in percentage of people living in cities
c. change in Seoul's population
d. change in average life expectancy
e. per capita GDP in dollars (before)
f. Seoul's current population
g. the year Seoul was founded
h. people who have bought their own apartments

The author's overall point of view of Seoul's rapid urbanization is **positive / neutral / negative**.

C What do these phrases/sentences from the article refer to or mean? Discuss with a partner.

1. paragraph 3: *The explosive energy of my generation . . .*
2. paragraph 4: *You can't understand urbanization in isolation from economic development.*
3. paragraph 7: *The chances are close to zero.*

Ask Answer

How have the residents of Seoul benefited from the city's rapid urbanization? Can you think of any disadvantages of such rapid growth? Compare a city near you to Seoul. How are they similar/different?

RAPID URBANIZATION: A Case Study

▶ There is no single model for how to manage rapid urbanization, but there are hopeful examples. One is Seoul, the capital of South Korea.

Between 1960 and 2000 Seoul's population grew from fewer than three million to ten million. South Korea, once one of the world's poorest countries with a per capita GDP of less than $100, became richer than some countries in Europe. The speed of the transformation shows. Driving into Seoul on the highway along the Han River, you pass an area of large concrete apartment blocks. They may not be very interesting on the outside, but as urban planner Yeong-Hee Jang put it, life inside "is so warm and convenient."

Seoul was a "planned city" from the start. The site was chosen as the capital in 1394. Its location, with the Han River to the south and a large mountain to the north, offered good protection from the northern winds. For five centuries it stayed a closed-off city of a few hundred thousand people. Then the twentieth century changed everything.

World War II and then the Korean War, which South Korea agreed to stop fighting in 1953, brought more than a million people into Seoul. They wanted to improve their lives. The "explosive energy of my generation," says Hong-Bin Kang, a former vice mayor who now runs Seoul's history museum, dates from this period. So does South Korea's population explosion, which happened due to rapid improvements in public health and nutrition.[1]

Over the years, Korean companies grew stronger. Central to the process, which created corporations like Samsung and Hyundai, were the men and women coming into Seoul to work in its new factories and educate themselves at its universities. "You can't understand urbanization in isolation[2] from economic development," says economist Kyung-Hwan Kim of Sogang University. The growing city enabled economic growth, which paid for the infrastructure that helped the city handle the country's growing population.

If you lived in old Seoul, north of the Han River, in the 1970s and 1980s, you watched an entirely new Seoul rise on the south bank, in the area called Kangnam. Over the years an increasing share of the population has been able to make money and live better due to an improving economy. And because the inhabitants of Seoul have been able to make more money, today half of them have been able to buy their own apartments.

Today Seoul is one of the densest[3] cities (twenty-four million in the metropolitan area) in the world. It has millions of cars but also an excellent subway system. The streets are busy with commerce and crowded with pedestrians. Life has gotten much better for Koreans as the country has gone from 28% urban in 1961 to 83% today. Life expectancy has increased from 51 years to 79. Korean boys now grow 6 inches (over 15 centimeters) taller than they used to.

South Korea's experience can't be easily copied, but it does prove that a poor country can urbanize successfully and incredibly fast. In the late 1990s Kyung-Hwan Kim worked for the UN in Nairobi, advising African cities on their difficult financial problems. "Every time I visited one of these cities I asked myself, What would a visiting expert have said to Koreans in 1960?" he says. "Would he have imagined Korea as it was fifty years later? The chances are close to zero."

[1] **nutrition** the foods that you take into your body (and how they influence your health)
[2] **in isolation (from)** separately (from)
[3] **dense** containing a lot of people or things in a small area; crowded

Urban renewal in Seoul created recreation space around Cheonggyecheon Stream.

Video

destruction the state of being destroyed
drought a long period of time in which no rain falls
soil the substance on the surface of the Earth in which plants grow; dirt
stunt to prevent something from growing as much as it should

A Read this information in preparation for watching the video. Use your dictionary to look up any unfamiliar words.

Nomads are people who move from place to place rather than living in one place all the time. In the open **steppe** of northern Mongolia, **herding** nomads **migrate** in search of food and resources, moving based on **climate** changes.

A *ger*, a tent used by Mongolian nomads, outside Mongolia's captial

B The video is about nomads giving up their lives and moving to the cities. Choose the main cause for these migrations. Then watch segment 1 and check your prediction.

weather changes on the steppe
job opportunities in the city
better housing in the city
a lack of interest in herding

C Watch segment 2 and complete the flow charts.

1. ____________ change → partly drives ____________
2. hard ____________ → drought conditions → hurts animals → forces nomads ____________
3. global warming → ____________ days are increasing
4. drought conditions → dry the ____________ → stunt the ____________ of vegetation → not enough to ____________ the animals

D Read this passage from the video. Match the underlined words to their definitions below.

There are still an (1) estimated thirty-three million (2) livestock in Mongolia, more than ten times the number of people. [One nomad named] Basanjav says he wants his children to (3) maintain the tradition of herding. He says his father was a herder and that it's important that his grandchildren (4) continue in the same footsteps. But the (5) odds that his grandchildren will grow up to be nomadic herders and continue this proud Mongolian tradition are becoming increasingly uncertain.

___ a. likelihood
___ b. animals such as cows and sheep
___ c. approximate
___ d. to do the same thing someone did before you
___ e. to preserve

Ask Answer Think about where your grandparents and parents have lived and the jobs they've had. Are you continuing in their footsteps? Why or why not? What are the odds that your children will have a better life than you?

Writing

Write a Summary

A Read this summary of the video on page 32. Then answer the questions.

Global warming has brought an increase in extreme weather events worldwide. In Mongolia, this is especially true, where average temperatures have risen about two degrees over the last sixty years. Mongolians are used to extreme temperatures, but the changes in climate have been more extreme than ever and that has been disastrous for the nomadic people and their way of life. Nowadays winters see heavier snowfalls and the rains in the summer are much less frequent than they used to be. This is a problem because the drought conditions have dried up the soil so much that the vegetation is dying out. The nomads' livestock cannot survive without enough to eat. Without healthy livestock, many nomads have been forced to give up their traditional nomadic lifestyle and move to the city. Because of this trend, global warming may ultimately lead to the destruction of the nomadic way of life.

1. What is the main idea and the conclusion of the paragraph? Underline each sentence.
2. What kind of information did the writer give to move from the main idea to the conclusion?

B Now look back at the article on page 31 and choose an answer to each question. You will use these sentences to start and end your summary.

1. What is the main idea of the article? (paragraph 1) Between 1960 and 2000 . . .
   a. South Korea became more urbanized and the quality of life declined.
   b. South Korea went from being a poor, rural-based economy to a successful urban one.
2. What does the writer conclude? (paragraph 7) A poor country . . .
   a. needs to grow slowly and carefully.
   b. can urbanize successfully and incredibly fast.

C How did the author move from the main idea to the conclusion? What kind of information did the author give? Follow these steps.

1. Use some of these key words to help you find important information and underline it in the article.

wars	education	corporations	infrastructure
housing	transportation	street life	overall health

2. Decide which information you want to include in your summary and then read the Writing Strategy.

Writing Strategy

Guidelines on Summary Writing A summary is a shorter account of an original text. It gives a reader a general idea of the text's content. When writing your summary . . .

1. Don't copy the author's ideas exactly. Rephrase the language with your own words.
2. Don't insert your own opinions into it.
3. Don't assume your audience already knows about the topic. (You may need to "state the obvious.")

D Use the information in Exercises **B** and **C** and the Writing Strategy to write your summary. Use a separate piece of paper. When you finish, exchange papers with a partner and read their summary. Was your partner's summary clear and concise?

Speaking

A Read this information about life in rural areas fifty years ago and today. What changes have occurred? Discuss with a partner.

In 2007, it was reported that for the first time in history more than half the global population lived in cities as opposed to rural areas.

FIFTY YEARS AGO

- The average farm was owned and operated by one family. Each farm required a large number of strong men and women to grow enough food to support the family.
- Many young people went directly to work after they graduated from high school.
- Several generations of a family lived and stayed in the village.
- Men and women got married within the same or nearby communities.

TODAY

- Farms are operated by large corporations. Modern farming uses machines and much less human labor.
- Young people need to get a college degree to succeed in the workplace and often leave home to study.
- The younger generations move to bigger cities to look for work.
- It can be harder to find a suitable partner in a small town.

B There are many factors that "push" a person to leave a small town and "pull" a person to migrate to a big city. Read the factors below. Brainstorm with a partner and add others on a separate piece of paper.

PUSH FACTORS (from a smaller town)	PULL FACTORS (to a bigger city)
Not enough jobs	*Better job opportunities*

C You and your partner are urban planners. Come up with a plan for reversing rural flight (the movement from rural areas to a big city).

- Look at your push and pull factors. Choose one to work on.
- On a separate piece of paper, come up with at least three ideas to address the problem.

D Find another pair and take turns presenting your ideas.

Unlike the cities, the rural district is not crowded with young people seeking work. To attract young workers back to the countryside, we propose. . .

Expanding Your Fluency

A These are photos of a city that has gone through rapid urbanization. Look at the photos and answer the questions with a partner.

1. The name of the city pictured is Astana. Where do you think it is located?
2. What do you think it is known for?
3. What symbol is this city associated with? What does the symbol mean?
4. Do you think this is a livable city? Why or why not?
5. What kinds of things do you think the city's inhabitants do in their free time?
6. What would you be interested in doing there?

B Work with a partner to create a short ad that will be used to attract visitors to Astana. Use some of these words in your ad.

community	district	global	livable	transformation
cosmopolitan	dynamic	infrastructure	metropolitan	urbanization

C Join another pair and take turns reading your ads. What do you like about each one? Why?

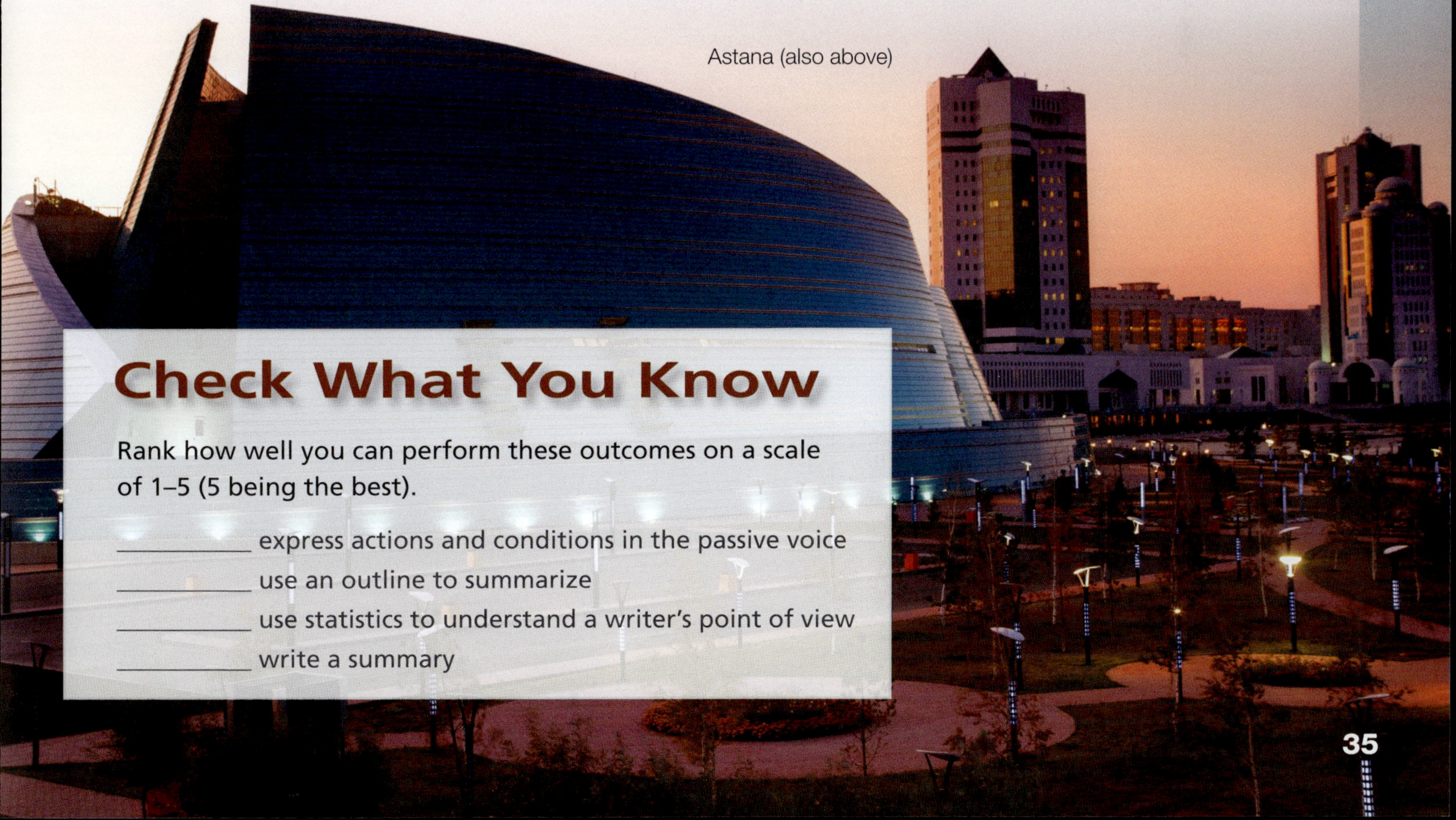

Astana (also above)

Check What You Know

Rank how well you can perform these outcomes on a scale of 1–5 (5 being the best).

__________ express actions and conditions in the passive voice
__________ use an outline to summarize
__________ use statistics to understand a writer's point of view
__________ write a summary

4 Being Yourself

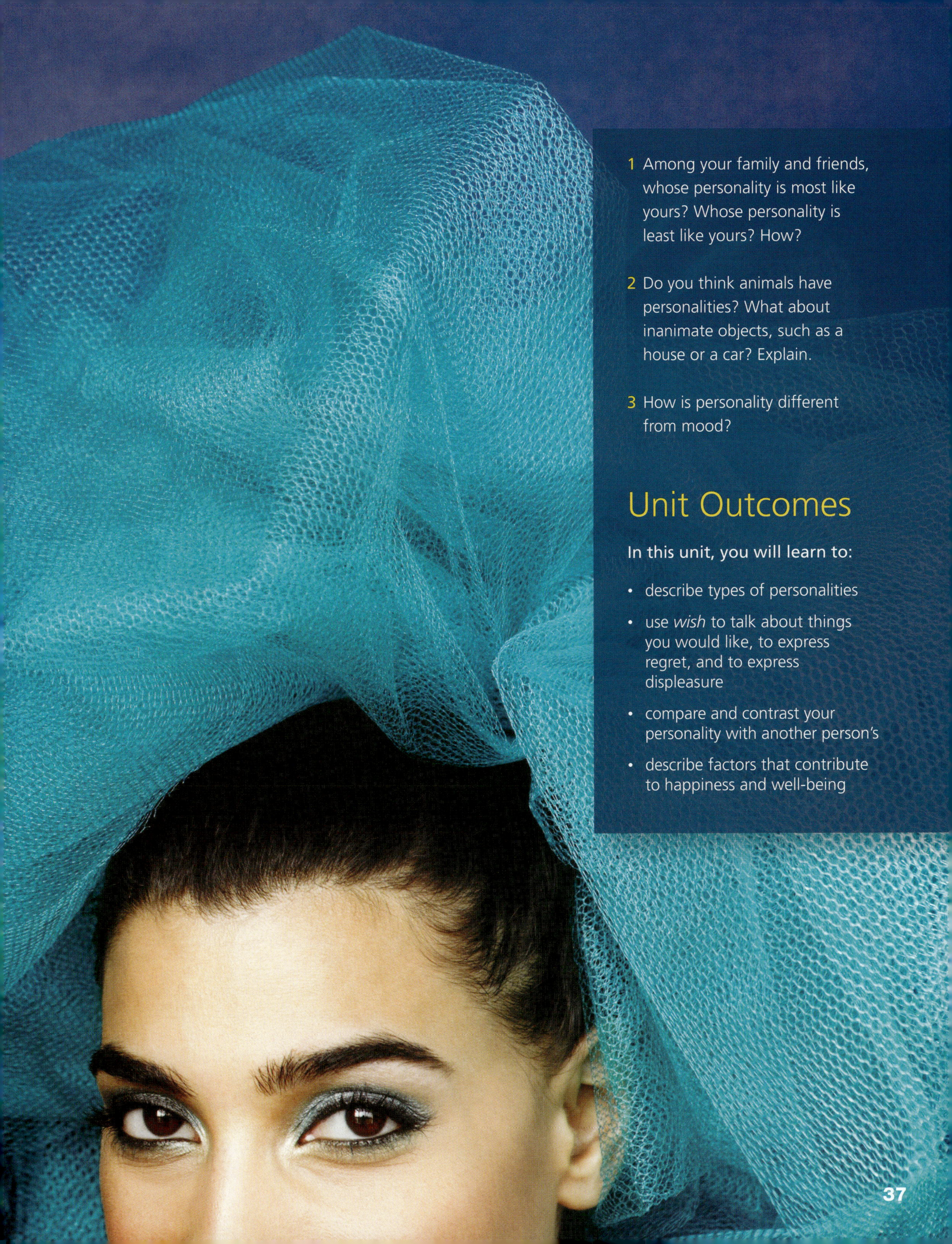

1 Among your family and friends, whose personality is most like yours? Whose personality is least like yours? How?

2 Do you think animals have personalities? What about inanimate objects, such as a house or a car? Explain.

3 How is personality different from mood?

Unit Outcomes

In this unit, you will learn to:

- describe types of personalities
- use *wish* to talk about things you would like, to express regret, and to express displeasure
- compare and contrast your personality with another person's
- describe factors that contribute to happiness and well-being

Vocabulary

affectionate loving and warm
ambitious very motivated to succeed
demanding difficult; insisting that something be done your way
get along (with someone) to have a friendly relationship with someone else
idealistic hopeful; believing in the best
innovative creative; original; inventive; new
picky critical; hard to please; choosy
pushover a person who is easily influenced by others
reserved keeping one's own feelings hidden
sensible logical; realistic
stubborn inflexible; unwilling to change your mind
supportive helpful and kind to those in need
thorough careful; detailed
upbeat positive and cheerful

Innovators: Steve Wozniak (left) and Steve Jobs, inventors of Appl

Usage: It's common to strengthen or soften personality adjectives using modifiers. Words like *really, pretty, so,* and *such* emphasize a word. (*She's pretty upbeat. He's such a pushover.*) It's common to soften negative words that describe people (e.g., *demanding, picky*) with modifiers like *kind of, sort of, a bit, a little,* and *somewhat.*

A With your class, look at the six personality types below. Match each type (A–F) with a description (1–6). More than one answer is possible.

_______ 1. is motivated to succeed
_______ 2. likes to fix all mistakes
_______ 3. likes caring for others
_______ 4. sees only the best side of things
_______ 5. loves taking risks
_______ 6. is studious and thoughtful

A. The Perfectionist sensible and thorough, but can be picky	**B. The Nurturer** affectionate and supportive, but can be a pushover	**C. The Go-Getter** ambitious and upbeat, but can be demanding
D. The Romantic idealistic and innovative, but can be impractical	**E. The Philosopher** patient and wise, but can seem reserved	**F. The Daredevil** daring and self-confident, but can be stubborn

B Read about the six personality types. Then answer the questions with a partner.

1. Which personality types might get along well with each other? Which might not? Why?
2. Which personality types best describe you? Choose two. Which one least describes you? Explain your choices. How similar are you to your partner?
3. Think of someone you admire; it can be someone you know or someone famous. Which personality type(s) describe that person? How do you compare to that person?

Grammar

bully using one's strength or power to hurt or frighten others

tolerant accepting and open-minded

Making Wishes		
	Real Situation	**Ideal Situation**
❶ **about the present**	I'**m** kind of short.	I wish (that) I **were** taller.
	I **don't speak** French.	I wish (that) I **spoke** French.
	She **has to leave** the party now.	She wishes (that) she **didn't have to leave**.
❷ **about the past**	I **was** careless on the exam.	I wish (that) I **had been** more thorough!
❸ **with *would***	We can't hear the teacher.	We wish (that) the teacher **would speak** louder so we could hear him.

Use *wish* to . . .
❶ talk about something you would like. In the *that* clause, the verb is in a past form.
❷ express regret about something that happened. In the *that* clause, the verb is in the past perfect.
❸ express displeasure in the moment with something or someone and to say that you want it to change.

For *be*, use *were* with both singular and plural subjects. In everyday spoken English, *was* is also used.

Pop singer Lady Gaga (right) started an organization called the Born This Way Foundation. As a teenager, she was bullied by neighborhood kids and classmates. The experience affected her deeply and influenced who she is today. The goals of her foundation are to discourage bullying and encourage people to be supportive and accepting of others.

A Read the information above about Lady Gaga. Then do the following:

a. Complete sentences 1–5 with the correct form of the verb in parentheses. In some cases, more than one option is possible.

b. Check answers with a partner. Which of the comments do you agree with or relate to? Why?

@JustMagical I was kind of a shy, reserved kid. I wish this foundation (1. be) __________ around when I was in high school! 7:38pm • 3 Apr

@tumtumtree72 Lady Gaga is being a little idealistic. I wish people (2. be) __________ kinder to each other, but usually they're not. It's human nature. 7:42pm • 3 Apr

@dudberry I love her idea. I wish more people (3. think) __________ like Lady Gaga! And I wish she (had) (4. create) __________ this foundation sooner! I wish more parents (5. teach) __________ their kids to be respectful and tolerant of others. 7:50pm • 3 Apr

B Discuss the questions.

1. Do you think your personality has been shaped by events in your life? Explain.
2. What about your personality do you like the most? What parts do you wish were different?
3. What's something you wish you had or hadn't done in the past? Why?

Listening

be hard on (someone) to treat someone in a severe or unkind way
lab partner in a science class like biology or chemistry, the student you work with in the laboratory to do certain experiments or exercises
work (something) out to find a solution to a problem

A You are going to hear a college student named Alana talk about a chemistry class she is taking. Have you ever taken a chemistry class? Describe it. Did you like it? Why or why not? Discuss with a partner.

B Listen as Alana talks to a friend. Then discuss the questions with a partner.

1. In general, how would you say Alana is doing in school? What kind of student would you say she is? Why?
2. How do you think Alana feels about her chemistry class: upbeat, confused, hopeful, overwhelmed?

TIP Notice how these expressions are used by the speakers: *It's stressing me out.* and *It's driving me crazy.* What feeling(s) do these expressions communicate?

C Read the statements. Then listen again and circle the correct answer.

1. Alana **is / isn't** happy with her most recent chemistry test grade.
   Reason: ____________________
2. Overall, Alana really **likes / dislikes** her chemistry class.
   Reason: ____________________
3. Alana wishes she didn't have to work with a **teacher / lab partner**.
   Reason: ____________________
4. Alana feels that her teacher **has / hasn't** been very supportive and helpful.
   Reason: ____________________
5. Alana plans to **do more / take a break from** schoolwork tonight.
   Reason: ____________________
6. The man encourages Alana to **sleep / study more** tonight.
   Reason: ____________________

D Listen again and give a reason for each statement in Exercise **C**.

E Compare answers in Exercises **C** and **D** with a partner. Then summarize what Alana's problem is. If you were in Alana's situation, what would you do?

Connections

A Get into a group of three. Read the information and the three profiles below. Then answer these questions:

1. What problem is the team having? Why aren't they getting along?
2. In general, what sort of personality type(s) would you say each person has?

You work for an international magazine that's published on the first of each month. Your team is responsible for next month's magazine cover and the main article. You are behind schedule because you are all having difficulty working with each other.

project manager You're responsible for getting the project done well and on time. You try to be supportive of your colleagues, but you're feeling a little annoyed with both of them at the moment. For example, you often ask the photographer for one kind of photo, and then he/she gives you something else. You wish he/she listened better. Having to do things over and over is slowing everything down and costing money. The designer has good ideas, though he/she is a bit reserved. You wish he/she would defend his/her ideas more.

photographer You're trying to take innovative, interesting photos for this month's main article and cover, but the project manager keeps telling you to change them. Sure, you don't follow instructions *exactly*. As an artist, you need to be creative in your photography. You wish the project manager were a little more flexible and a little less picky! You've also argued with the designer about which photo should appear on next month's cover. You want one thing, and the designer insists on something else. You wish that he/she weren't so stubborn.

designer You're responsible for the layout of the images on the magazine cover and in the main article. In your opinion, the photographer has taken some interesting photos for next month's cover, but many are impractical. They just won't fit and look good. You really hate arguing and wish the photographer would be reasonable. You've tried talking to the project manager about this, but he/she can be such a pushover and always does whatever the photographer wants. You wish the manager took your side once in a while.

B With your group, decide which role each group member will take. On your own, think about these questions:

1. What do you want from the two other team members?
2. What can you suggest to improve the team's working relationship so that you can complete your project on time?

C Imagine that you and your colleagues are meeting to discuss the problem. Take turns explaining in your own words what issues you're having with the others on your team and what you'd like from them. Together, try to reach a compromise. Make a plan for how you're going to finalize the cover and the main article.

D What compromise did your group reach and how are you all going to move forward? Share your plan with another group. Were your ideas similar?

> Carlos, you've taken some great photos, but I'm worried that they won't look good on the cover. I really wish we didn't have to argue about this. Paloma, you're the project manager, what do you suggest?

Reading

A Make a list of three things that make you happy. Then get into a group of four and compare your answers. Were any of your answers the same? Share your results with the class.

B Read only the title and the first paragraph of the article. Then guess where the happiest place in Asia, Europe, and the Americas is. Why do you think people there are happy? Compare your ideas with a partner's. Then read the rest of the article to check your ideas.

C Locate the word or phrase in the paragraph noted in the chart. In the same paragraph, find the synonym or antonym of the word or phrase and write it in the chart.

Paragraph	Word or phrase	Synonym	Antonym
1	satisfaction (*noun*)	________________	unhappiness
2	peace of mind (*noun*)	________________	danger
3	honesty (*noun*)	truthfulness	________________
3	tolerance (*noun*)	acceptance	________________

D Complete the graphic organizer with information from the article. List the country or region and the reasons why these are the happiest places on Earth. Then summarize the findings with a partner.

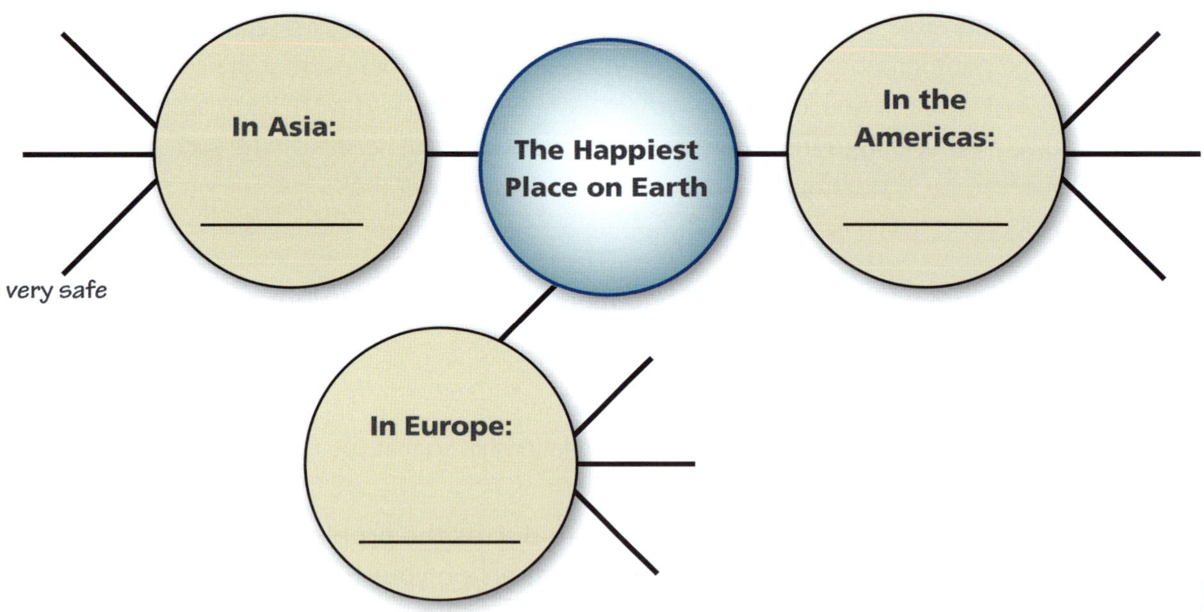

E Discuss the questions with a partner.

1. Did any of the findings in the article surprise you?
2. How does your country or region compare to those listed in the article? In general, would you say that people where you live are happy? Why or why not? Which of the "happiness factors" in Exercise **D** do you wish were more common in your country?

SECRETS of the Happiest Places on Earth

For much of the last decade, author and explorer Dan Buettner has traveled to places where people live longest and where they claim to get the greatest satisfaction from their lives. Recently, Buettner visited different continents and worked with leading researchers to identify the happiest place on each. Where are these places, why are people there happier than others, and what can we learn from these people about finding contentment in our own lives? Dan Buettner's findings may surprise you.

Asia

Most people believe the happiest place in Asia is Bhutan. It's not. According to research, it's Singapore, for a variety of reasons. First, Singapore is very safe. A woman can walk alone at night without the fear of being harmed. Children can spend time at the playground and parents don't have to worry about them being taken. This peace of mind is very important when it comes to happiness. Also, 90% of Singaporeans own their own home—another source of security. There are also tax incentives[1] to live close to your aging parents, so seniors are taken care of at a higher level. Research shows that we're happier when we socialize, and we get the most satisfaction from socializing with our families.

Europe

Worldwide, happiness correlates[2] very strongly with equality. Countries that have a very narrow gap between the richest and the poorest people are a lot happier than those where only a few people make a lot of money and the others don't make much. In Denmark, a CEO only makes about three times as much as an average worker, whereas in other countries, CEOs make many thousands of times as much as a typical employee. Research also shows that honesty and trust strongly correlate with happiness. Places where people are honest and where there is low governmental corruption tend to be happier. Tolerance also contributes to contentment. Knowing that you won't face discrimination because of your gender, age, religious beliefs, or ethnicity makes people happier. All three of these things promote a sense of well-being and are present in Denmark, making it the happiest place in Europe.

The Americas

Buettner also looked at Nuevo León, the happiest region of Mexico, which was the happiest country in the American hemisphere when he did his research. Something interesting is going on in this part of Mexico. Research shows that worldwide, religious people are happier than nonreligious people, and for more than 80% of those in Nuevo León, religious faith tops their list of values. Family is also extremely important in Nuevo León; this includes not only moms, dads, and children; but also aunts, uncles, cousins, and grandparents. Having a large extended family does some helpful things, such as providing a financial safety net,[3] which is a defense against stress. Of course, people in Mexico do suffer from all kinds of difficult things in their lives, but a large family can be supportive and help a person get through the challenging times. Also, there are many weddings, birthday parties, and other family events that people attend; this means that residents of Nuevo León are getting lots of social interaction, which contributes a lot to personal happiness.

[1] **tax incentive** a decrease in the amount of tax one must pay
[2] **correlate** to have a close connection to something else
[3] **safety net** money you can rely on if you get into a difficult financial situation

Singapore, one of the happiest places in the world

Video

longevity long life
obesity the state of being very overweight
sedentary inactive; sitting a lot
unplug to relax and do nothing
wear the pants to be in control
zeal a strong enthusiasm for something

A **Discuss the questions with a partner.**

1. Who is the oldest person you know? How has he or she managed to live so long?
2. Researcher David McLain visited three "cultures of longevity." What do you know about the three places in Exercise **B**? Why do you think people there are living so long?

B **Read the information below and then watch the video. Complete each aging fact. Then match the reasons (a–e) with a place. A reason can be used more than once.**

Place	Aging fact	Reason(s) people live so long
Sardinia, Italy	Men there live ______ women.	
Okinawa, Japan	Okinawa is home to the ______ on Earth.	
Loma Linda, USA	Seventh-day Adventists outlive other Americans by ______ years.	

Reasons people live so long:

a. They have active lifestyles.
b. They regularly take a day off.
c. They have lower stress levels (especially the men).
d. They socialize with family or friends often.
e. They have a healthy diet.

Did you know?

On average, women tend to live five years longer than men.

C **Compare answers in Exercise B with a partner. Explain what information from the video helped you choose your answers for each place.**

D **In each place, is the culture of longevity changing? Watch the video again. Mark *yes* or *no* and list the reason(s).**

Sardinia yes / no reason: ________________
Okinawa yes / no reason: ________________
Loma Linda yes / no reason: ________________

E **Discuss these questions with a partner.**

1. Why are the people in each place living so long? Were any of the reasons for longevity the same?
2. Which factors mentioned in the video were also mentioned in the reading on page 43? What does this tell us about the connection between happiness and long life?

Speaking

A Complete the survey by marking how you feel on the scale. Are you closer to one side or the other, or are you in the middle? Be prepared to explain your responses.

Life Satisfaction Survey

I'm feeling stressed out by life at the moment.	1	2	3	4	5	I'm pretty upbeat about most things in my life.
I wish I lived somewhere else.	1	2	3	4	5	I like where I live.
My family drives me crazy.	1	2	3	4	5	I get along well with my family members.
I wish I were a more social person.	1	2	3	4	5	I have a decent social life.
I wish school wasn't so hard./ I wish I had a different job.	1	2	3	4	5	I like the school I go to or the job I do.
I'd like to change some things about my appearance.	1	2	3	4	5	I'm satisfied with my appearance.

B Get together with a partner and do the following:

1. On a separate piece of paper, draw a diagram like the one shown. Make it large enough to fit your responses and your partner's responses.
2. With your partner, compare your responses to the survey in Exercise **A**. Record your answers and your partner's answers in the diagram. Remember to explain your answers. Take notes on what your partner tells you.
3. Discuss the questions. Use the language in the Speaking Strategy.
    - In general, how similar are you to each other?
    - Are there things your partner wishes he or she could change?
    - What advice can you suggest?

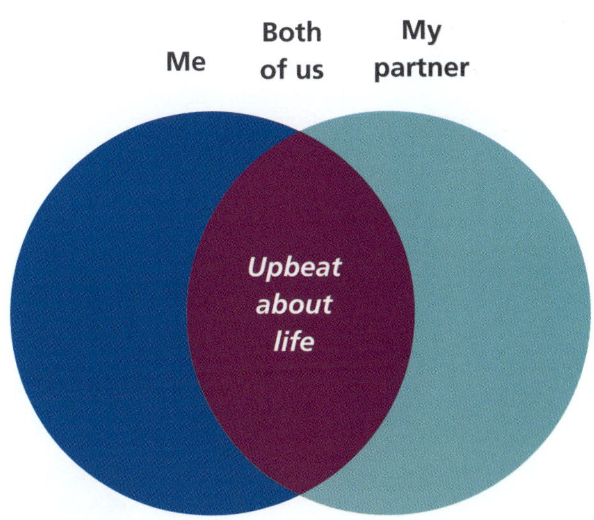

Speaking Strategy

Making General Comparisons

We're fundamentally/completely different.
We're kind of/sort of/somewhat similar.
We're very similar./We're pretty much alike.
We're virtually/practically/almost identical.

Making Specific Comparisons

I'm pretty upbeat about most things in my life.
Yeah, me too./So am I.
I'm kind of in the middle.
Not me. I'm feeling really stressed out by school these days.

Writing

Compare and Contrast Yourself with Another Person

A Read the paragraphs. Then answer the questions below with the same partner you worked with on page 45.

For the most part, my partner Mayumi and I are very similar. For example, we're **both** pretty upbeat people. She's almost always in a good mood and **so am I. Like me,** she rarely gets stressed out or lets little things get her down. Mayumi gets along well with her family members and **the same is true for** me. Mayumi is close to her younger sister, and I'm especially close to my mom and brother.

Both Mayumi and I are also very social people and enjoy hanging out with our friends; **however,** we don't really like doing the same things. She loves going out to clubs on the weekends. I, **on the other hand**, prefer to relax or play video games with my friends. Mayumi also goes out a lot and has a pretty decent social life, **whereas** I wish I had more free time. Going to school and working a part-time job make that difficult, though. Despite these minor differences, Mayumi and I are very similar.

Start the composition with a clear topic sentence that states generally how you and your partner compare.

Illustrate each point of similarity or difference with extra facts or information.

End with a sentence that summarizes how you and your partner compare.

1. How are the writer and Mayumi similar? How are they different?
2. Which boldfaced words or phrases compare? Which contrast? Answer on a separate piece of paper.

B You are going to write a short composition comparing yourself to your partner. Follow these steps.

1. Outline your ideas.
   a. Start with a topic sentence that states generally how you and your partner compare.
   b. Using the diagram and the notes you took on page 45, identify three points of similarity or difference that support your topic sentence.
   c. Illustrate each point of similarity or difference with extra facts or information.
   d. Conclude with a sentence that summarizes how you and your partner compare.
2. Use your outline to write your composition. Remember to use the boldfaced words and phrases from Exercise **A**.

C Exchange papers with a different partner and read the other student's composition. Does it achieve the four things listed in Exercise **B1** (a–d) and use the boldfaced words and phrases?

Expanding Your Fluency

A Take two slips of paper. On each, write a wish about your personality. Then give them to your teacher.

> I wish that I were more ambitious.
>
> I wish I was a little less demanding.
>
> I wish I weren't such a perfectionist sometimes.
>
> I wish I were more supportive with friends.

Rub the lamp and you will be granted three wishes.

B Your teacher will now give you two slips of paper. Find who wrote each wish. When you find the person, ask him or her to explain why he/she made that wish. Take notes on what the person tells you.

Do you wish you were more ambitious?

Yeah, I wrote that.

Why did you make that wish?

Sometimes I lack confidence . . .

C Get together with a partner and describe the two wishes you learned about. Of the four wishes you two have in total, which <u>one</u> would you grant if you could? Why? Share your answer with the class.

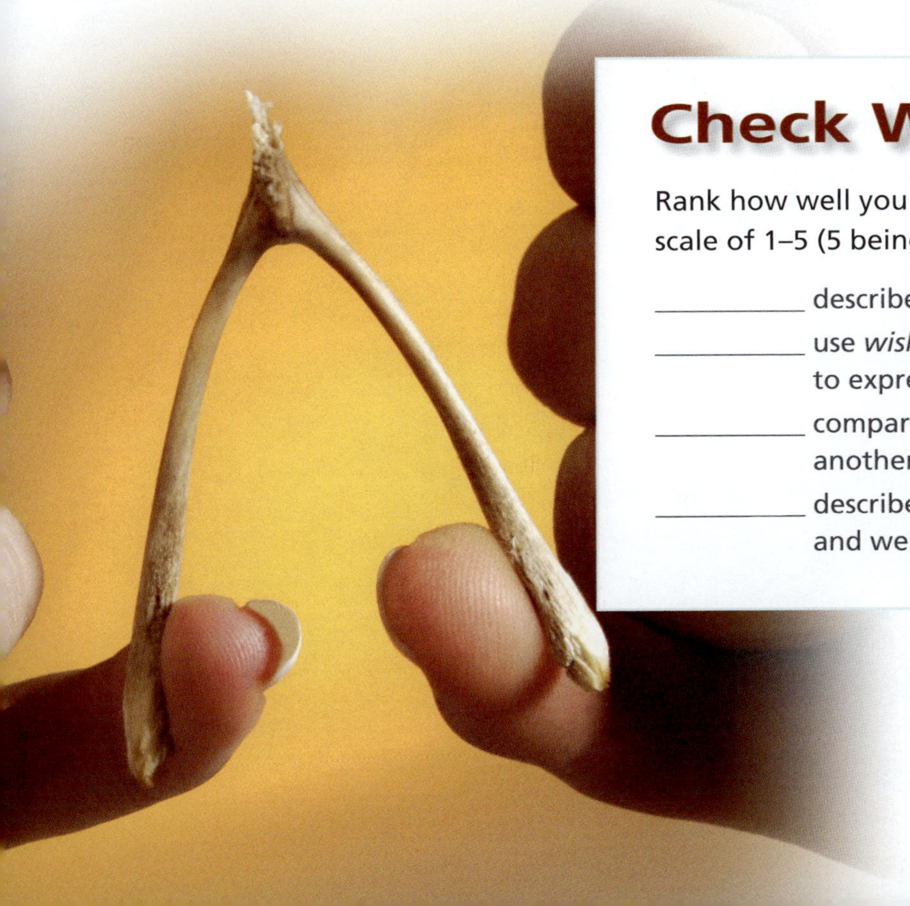

Check What You Know

Rank how well you can perform these outcomes on a scale of 1–5 (5 being the best).

__________ describe types of personalities

__________ use *wish* to talk about things you would like, to express regret, and to express displeasure

__________ compare and contrast your personality with another person's

__________ describe factors that contribute to happiness and well-being

Make a wish and then pull on the wishbone.

5 Mystery Solved!

1 Where do you think this statue is located? How do you think it got there? Do you think it's mysterious? Why or why not?

2 What is the strangest animal you have ever seen or read about?

3 Name three places on Earth that are considered mysterious. Which one would you most like to visit? Why?

Unit Outcomes

In this unit, you will learn to:

- use modals of possibility in the past, present, and future
- speculate about mysteries
- refute ideas
- use *wh-* questions to help you plan a story

Vocabulary

absorb to reduce the force of something; soak up or take in
aggressive acting in an angry or violent manner
case a situation or incident
clue something that helps you find the answer to a problem
mystery something that is difficult to understand or explain
observation the act of carefully watching someone or something
solve to find an answer to a problem or crime
surroundings the immediate area around you
theory a formal idea that is intended to explain something
twist to turn
uncover to discover something previously unknown or hidden
unharmed not hurt or damaged in any way

Usage: *Twist* is a verb, but it can also be used as a noun as it is below in **bold**. What is the meaning of that usage of *twist*?

A Use words from the list to complete the two stories below. Work with a partner.

Animal Mysteries

Sam the Parrot

Parrots are popular pets because they're friendly and intelligent.

Sandy, who recently married Ken, has a parrot named Sam. Sam was a loving pet . . . until about six months ago. He became (1) _______ and started biting Ken. Sandy can't understand why Sam has changed from a loving pet to an attack bird. There are few (2) _______ to explain Sam's behavior.

Can you help Sandy by solving this (3) _______?

PARROT FACTS:

- Parrots can "talk" (say short words) like people do. They do this to fit into new (4) _______.
- Parrots form close pair bonds. In the wild, a parrot couple can stay together for decades.
- We know that parrots feel that "three's a crowd."

Acrobatic Cats

We all know from personal (5) _______ that when cats fall, they almost always land on their feet. There are stories of cats surviving long falls out of building windows virtually (6) _______.

There's a **twist** to this story, though. In a recent study, veterinarian Michael Garvey (7) _______ a mystery about cats. He discovered that cats that fall a longer distance have fewer injuries than cats that fall shorter distances.

CAT FACTS:

- When cats fall, the first thing they do is twist their heads around quickly to straighten their bodies.
- Then, they completely relax their bodies.
- Finally, they land on all four feet in order to (8) _______ the impact.

B Work with a partner and answer the two questions below. Come up with a theory for each mystery.

1. Why did Sam's behavior suddenly change?
2. Why do cats that fall shorter distances have more injuries?

Grammar

You're going to the zoo. You've agreed to meet Joe and Ann there at 9:45 a.m. Read the sentences in the chart below to see what happens.

Modals of Possibility in the Past, Present, and Future		
	Present/Future	**Past**
strong certainty	(9:45 a.m.) Joe's not here yet. He **must** be on his way, though.	(9:45 a.m.) Ann's not here yet. She **must have** left her house late.
weaker certainty	(9:50 a.m.) He's still not here. He **could/may/might** be stuck in traffic.	(9:50 a.m.) She's still not here. I **could have/may have/might have** told her the wrong time.
impossibility	(9:58 a.m.) He just got here. I **can't/ couldn't** be more relieved.	(the next day) Ann said she didn't see me at the zoo. She **couldn't have** looked very hard—I was there the whole time!

A Read about this animal mystery and then mark your answers below.

Possible causes of population decline: pollution, climate change, loss of habitat, rise in human population, disease

Animal Mystery: Frogs Disappearing

Scientists have observed something shocking among frog populations worldwide. Out of 6,000 frog species, one-third are facing massive decline. No one is certain why this is happening, but we do know that frogs are very sensitive to their surroundings—especially to changes in the air and water.

Here's what different people had to say about the situation:

1. "I was shocked to hear that most of the frogs in this area have died out. That just **can't / must** be true!"
2. "With all the research tools we have, I'm certain we can figure this out. There **might / must** be a simple answer to this mystery."
3. "I can't find any frogs today. At first, I thought they **might / might not** be hiding. But now I know that isn't true."
4. "It's pretty obvious that humans are at fault. We **couldn't have / must have** done something to damage the environment . . . and that's killing off the frogs."
5. "Some people say that dogs and cats killed all the frogs in this area, but that **could have / couldn't have** been the only cause."

B Why do you think that frogs are disappearing worldwide? Read the possible causes in Exercise **A**. Discuss each cause with a partner.

I think pollution could be one of the causes. It says that frogs are sensitive to . . .

Ask Answer

Are there any mysteries where you live that people can't explain? If so, what are they? Are there any clues or do you have any theories about them?

Listening

tow to pull something or someone by a rope tied to a vehicle

Talking about groups of animals
a herd of cattle
a pod of dolphins
a school of fish

A Look at the information in the box and the photo. You are going to hear a story about Erik. What do you think happened to Erik? Discuss with a partner.

B Listen to the news story about what happened to Erik. Complete the sentences below. You will not hear all of the answers.

1. where he surfs	*He surfs at ________.*
2. what the doctors expect	*They expect him to make a complete ________.*
3. why he was so far away	*He was ________ out to sea by a jet ski.*
4. what happened to him	*He was ________ by a ________.*
5. what happened to his surfboard	*The ________ bit it.*
6. who helped him	*A ________ of ________ helped him.*
7. how they helped him	*They ________ around him and ________ him.*

C Now listen to two friends talking about Erik. Complete the rest of the sentences in Exercise **B**.

D Listen and complete the expressions that express shock and disbelief/surprise.

Expressing shock	Expressing disbelief/surprise
This ________ as a complete shock.	I just ________ how scared he must have been.
I was ________ to hear the news . . .	________ that he was able to escape.

E Work with a partner. Close your books and practice retelling Erik's story. Use one of the expressions in Exercise **D** and some of the words below.

aggressive mystery observation twist unharmed

Ask Answer
Do you believe Erik's story? Why or why not?
Why do you think the dolphins helped Erik? Do you know any other stories where animals helped humans?

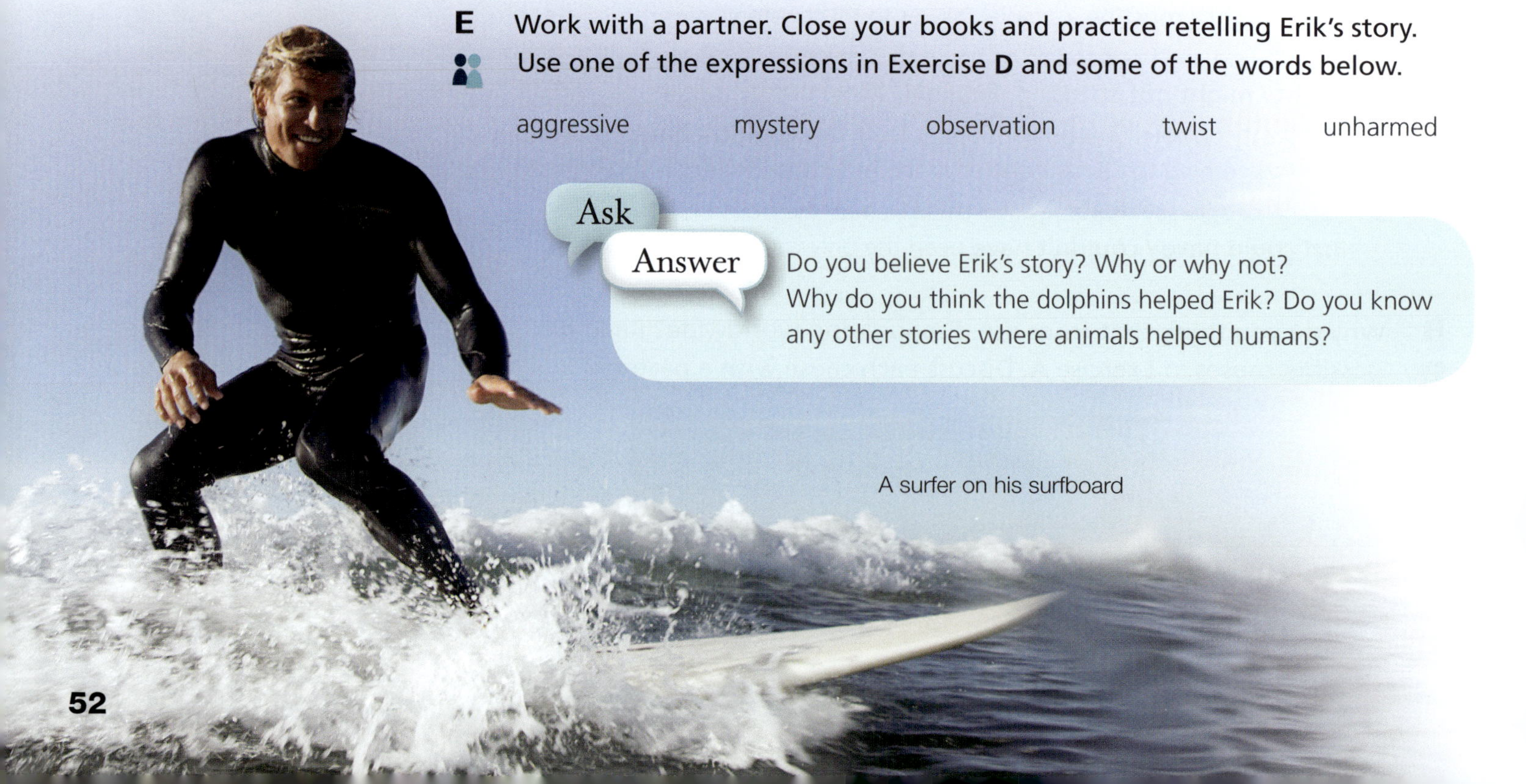

A surfer on his surfboard

Connections

A Look at the photo of trees and discuss the questions with a partner.

1. Something mysterious happened to these trees. What is your theory of what happened?
2. What else can you observe in the photo? What else can you see in the trees' surroundings?

B Now read the entry from Julio's travel diary about his visit to the area in the photo. Then discuss the questions with your partner.

Dec. 10 — Pakistan

I've just arrived in a town where they had ten years' worth of rain in one week! The town and its surroundings have been flooded. Thousands of people have lost their homes and it's been hard on the animals too. There's a strange twist to all this—all of the trees look so weird! They've been largely unharmed by the floods, but they're covered in something sticky that's killing them! I wonder what it could be.

1. What do you think is covering the trees? There are several theories. Discuss each one (as well as your own ideas) with your partner.

   ☐ tree fungus ☐ spider webs ☐ mosquito nets ☐ an art project ☐ other: ______

2. What do you think actually happened? Agree on the idea that you think best explains the mystery.

> I guess it could be mosquito nets, but actually, it looks more like . . .

C Work with your partner and prepare a presentation on poster paper that encourages people to save the trees. Your poster should include the following information (as well as your own art work):

1. Explain what the problem is. What is killing the trees?
2. How do you propose to solve the problem? Come up with a slogan for your solution—a phrase that captures people's attention.

D Present your ideas to the class. The class votes on the best presentation.

Speaking

bury to place something in a hole in the ground and cover it with dirt

cemetery a place where the bodies or ashes of the dead are buried

monument a large structure, usually made of stone, built to remind people of something

skeleton the frame of bones supporting a human or animal body

A Look at the photos below. Tell your partner what you know about them.

B Read the information about Stonehenge and crop circles. Which theory do you think is correct for each? Why do you feel less confident in the other theories?

Circular Mysteries of the World

STONEHENGE

Stonehenge is an ancient site made up of large stones arranged in a circle.

Constructed: 3100 BCE–1600 BCE

Builders: unknown

What is it? Theories:

1. Ancient people might have placed the stones carefully to use as a kind of calendar.
2. Scientists have discovered skeletons buried on the site. They think it may have been a cemetery.
3. Some of the skeletons have strange wounds. People may have come to Stonehenge to get medical treatment.
4. The nearby residents may have arranged the stones to create a monument of peace and unity.

CROP CIRCLES

Crop circles are large areas of flattened crops in the shape of various patterns.

First noticed: 1970s

Builders: unknown

How are they made? Theories:

1. Scientists wonder if strange weather patterns might have caused the circles to form.
2. Some say the patterns can easily be made using a rope and board to crush the crops.
3. Some claim that aliens created the circles as directions for an invasion of Earth.
4. Some scientists have suggested that you can create the patterns by "burning" the fields with lasers.

C Follow these steps with your partner.

1. Student A: State which Stonehenge theory you believe.
2. Student A: Take no more than one minute to refute the other theories. Use the Speaking Strategy to help you explain why the theories are wrong.
3. Student B: After Student A finishes, complete steps 1 and 2.
4. Students A and B: Discuss which arguments were most convincing.
5. Students A and B: Follow steps 1–4 with the crop circle theories.

Speaking Strategy

Refuting a Theory

Moderate

It's possible that ______.
However, it's more likely that ______ because . . .
I suppose that ______ could be true, but that's probably not the case because . . .

Stronger

It seems unlikely that . . .
I doubt (very much) that . . .
It's impossible that . . .
There's no chance that . . .

Video

archaeologist a person who studies people and societies of the past by examining their culture, architecture, tools, and other objects

complex a group of buildings designed for a particular purpose

loot to steal from shops and houses

settlement a place where people gather to build homes and live

withstand to survive or not give in to a force or action

A Match the words in the box with their antonym. Use your dictionary to help you.

isolated	novel	permanent	solitary

1. *temporary* ____________________
2. *easy to reach* ____________________
3. *unoriginal* ____________________
4. *together (with other things)* ____________________

B What do you think Stonehenge may have been used for? Think back to the answer you gave on page 54. Watch the video and complete the sentences.

According to an archaeologist, Stonehenge was not a / an (1) ______________ monument. People lived in (2) ______________ homes nearby and (3) ______________ their (4) ______________ at Stonehenge.

PRONUNCIATION

Is Michael Parker Pearson's accent American or British? How can you tell? For more on the differences between American English and British English, see p. 145.

C Watch the video about Stonehenge and a nearby settlement called Durrington Walls. Match each description with one of the locations.

	Stonehenge	**Durrington Walls**
1. has been looted.	☐	☐
2. was a large community.	☐	☐
3. is an obsession for Mr. Pearson, an archaeologist.	☐	☐
4. is located upstream.	☐	☐
5. is not a solitary, isolated place.	☐	☐
6. was where people lived.	☐	☐
7. was where people were buried.	☐	☐
8. is timeless.	☐	☐

D Each sentence has one error. Watch the video and correct the sentences.

1. Archaeologist Michael Parker Pearson has been digging around Stonehenge since 1999.
2. In 2006, he made a great discovery of many skeletons.
3. Durrington Walls may have contained dozens of houses.
4. It is estimated that 240 stones were placed at Stonehenge.

Ask Answer What do you think of Michael Parker Pearson's theory? Do you think Stonehenge is a mysterious place? Why or why not?

Reading

A Read the title and subtitle of the article and look at the map. Who do you think would visit Stonehenge 3,500 years ago? Tell a partner what you think.

B Find the word or phrase that matches the definition.

1. ______________ (paragraph 3) unusual and interesting, often because it comes from a distant country
2. ______________ (paragraph 4) to reduce the number of choices or ideas
3. ______________ (paragraph 5) data that represents a person's traits
4. ______________ (paragraph 7) made guesses about something
5. ______________ (paragraph 8) a disease caused by germs or bacteria

Amber beads

C Why does the writer mention these place names in the article? Read the article and make notes about each place on a separate piece of paper.

1. Mediterranean coast
2. Amesbury
3. English Channel

D What do scientists know about the boy with the amber necklace? What do those facts tell us about him? Read the article again and complete the chart.

Clue	What we know	What it tells us
Teeth		
Necklace		
Age		
Injuries		

Ask Answer Do you know of any places that contain mysteries like Stonehenge? Have the mysteries been solved? What clues were left?

The Boy with the **Amber Necklace**

3,500 years ago, Stonehenge was attracting visitors from all over the world. The question is: Who were they?

Stonehenge has long been a source of mystery and questions. Who built it? Why did they build it? How was it built? But today, advances in science are beginning to reveal information that could change the way we think about the ancient site. For instance, new evidence shows that Bronze Age[1] people traveled all the way from the Mediterranean coast—more than 500 miles (805 kilometers) away—to see the standing stones on Britain's Salisbury Plain.

One notable example of these Bronze Age visitors to Stonehenge is a 14- or 15-year-old boy buried outside the town of Amesbury, about 3 miles (5 kilometers) from Stonehenge. Chemical analysis of his teeth reveal that he came from somewhere in the Mediterranean region.

Discovered in 2005, the teen was buried about 3,550 years ago wearing a necklace of about 90 amber[2] beads. "Such exotic materials demonstrate that he was from one of the highest levels of society," said project archaeologist Andrew Fitzpatrick of Wessex Archaeology, a consulting firm based in Salisbury, England.

To determine that the teen wasn't a local, scientists from the British Geological[3] Survey (BGS) measured oxygen[4] and other substances in his teeth. The amounts of these substances change depending on an area's unique climate and geology. This information gets recorded in a person's teeth and can be used to narrow down their native region.

In the case of the boy with the amber necklace, it became clear that he wasn't originally from Stonehenge. Instead, his chemical profile matched that of a person from an area like the coastal Mediterranean. In short, scientists think he traveled to Stonehenge from a much warmer place.

The researchers were able to learn even more about the boy. Because he was so young, archaeologists suspect the boy traveled with an extended family group. "We think that the wealthiest people may have made these long-distance journeys in order to find rare and exotic materials, like amber. By doing these journeys, they probably also acquired great kudos,"[5] Wessex's Fitzpatrick noted.

Crossing the English Channel from mainland Europe—most likely by paddleboat—was probably one of the more challenging parts of this journey, he speculated.

The boy's skeleton bears no obvious injuries, suggesting he died of infection. He was buried near Stonehenge likely because of its significance at the time, experts say. The boy is just one of a number of burials near Stonehenge that show that the monument drew visitors from far and wide.

[1] **Bronze Age** the period of ancient human culture between 4000 and 1200 BCE
[2] **amber** a hard yellowish-brown substance used to make jewelry
[3] **geological** related to the study of the Earth's rocks, minerals, and surface
[4] **oxygen** a gas in the air that all humans, animals, and plants need to live
[5] **kudos** public admiration or recognition received when doing something

Writing

Recount a Story

A Read the letter from the Bronze Age. Then answer the questions.

Hi and greetings from Britain! May 17, 2000 BCE

After a weeklong journey from France, my family and I finally arrived in Britain three days ago. The trip could have been easier, but on the second day, a terrible storm slowed our channel crossing. . . . I've never seen such big waves! Fortunately, our boat was able to withstand the high winds and rough seas and we arrived exhausted, but unharmed. I've never been so happy to get somewhere in my life!

Our journey is just beginning, though. Tomorrow we head out for Stonehenge. It sounds like a mysterious place, but I really can't be sure. There are all these stones clustered together in different formations. We'll be staying nearby in Woodhenge. My mother says she must do some shopping while she's here—she wants to buy some amber stones for her . . .

1. Who do you think wrote it?
   a. a servant being taken with a family to Stonehenge
   b. a teenager traveling with his / her family to Stonehenge
   c. a merchant going to Stonehenge to buy exotic jewels to sell in his / her country
2. What do you think the purpose of this letter is?
   a. to describe the journey
   b. to give some practical advice
   c. to complain about something

B Imagine that you are living in ancient times, and you're making a trip to Stonehenge or another mysterious site. You are going to write a letter back home to a friend. Do the following:

1. Decide which mysterious site you are visiting, who you are, and why you're writing. (What is your purpose?) Use the ideas in Exercise **A** or ideas of your own.
2. Read the Writing Strategy. Then complete the organizer with details about your story.
3. Using your notes, write a letter of at least three paragraphs.

Writing Strategy

Using a Graphic Organizer to Help You Tell a Story

The graphic organizer to the right can help you to organize your thoughts before you write. By answering the *wh-* questions in the organizer, you force yourself to think about all the main details of your story.

1. Write the topic of your letter (trip to a mysterious site) in the middle of the circle.
2. Write *wh-* questions that relate to your topic. You will answer these questions in your letter.

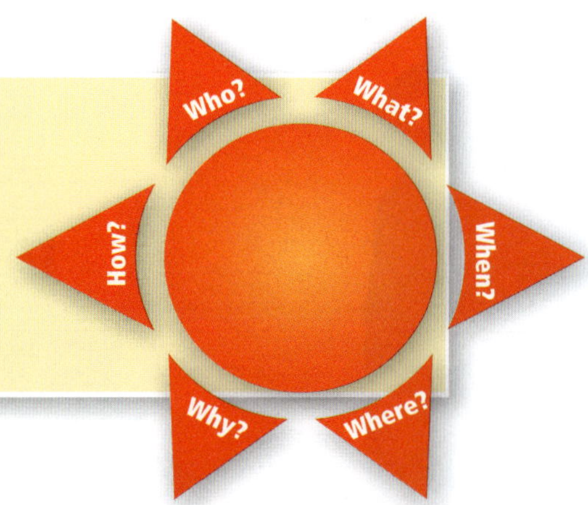

C Exchange letters with a partner.

1. Without looking at your partner's organizer, what are some of the questions that his or her letter answers? Do you have any unanswered questions?
2. What is the most interesting thing you learned from your partner's letter? The most surprising thing?

Expanding Your Fluency

A Choose one of the objects in the photos and complete the role-play below.

Archaeologist: You have made a fascinating discovery and are meeting a reporter to tell the world about your exciting discovery. Think about how you would answer the questions from the list.

Reporter: Ask the archaeologist about the object using the questions from the list. You can add some of your own questions to the list.

- Where did you find it?
- Who used it?
- Why is it important?

____

____

____

____

____

B Switch roles and do the role-play again with the other object.

Check What You Know

Rank how well you can perform these outcomes on a scale of 1–5 (5 being the best).

__________ use modals of possibility in the past, present, and future

__________ speculate about mysteries

__________ refute ideas

__________ use *wh-* questions to help you plan a story

6 New Horizons

1 What do you see? What do you think is happening in this photo?

2 What kinds of new discoveries do you think will be made in the future?

3 Flip through the unit quickly. What new possibilities will you be learning about in this unit? Which one looks most interesting to you?

Unit Outcomes

In this unit, you will learn to:

- make predictions using different future forms
- identify key words used to explain reasons
- describe skills needed to achieve future goals
- develop and write a counterargument

.97' 74° 45.76' 18
.31' 74° 45.72' 18
.29' 74° 45.49' 18
.26' 73° 35.12' 18
.90' 73° 38.29' 18
95' 73° 38.32' 18

Vocabulary

cutting-edge the most advanced or most exciting in a particular field

efficient able to do tasks successfully, without wasting time or energy

feasible possible

interact (with) to communicate as you work or spend time together with others

obsolete no longer necessary because something better has been invented

primitive simple; not well developed

take (something) for granted accept that something is true or normal without thinking about it

versatile able to be used for many different purposes

A What technologies did not exist a hundred years ago that we now take for granted? How have these things transformed people's lives? What would life be like without them? Discuss your answers with a partner.

B Look at the photos and describe what you see. Then use the vocabulary from the list to complete the profile below. Work with a partner.

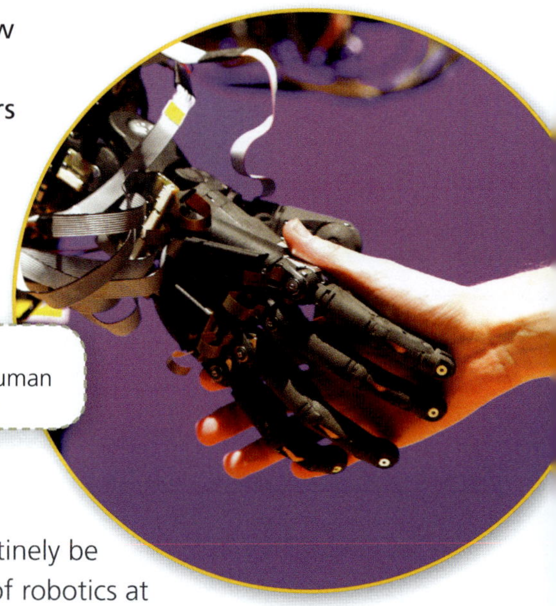

This robot mimics human gestures, such as shaking hands.

ROBOT REVOLUTION

Types of robots
android a robot that looks human
drone a robotic flying device

Robots are being created that can think, (1) ______________ with people, and even relate to people. Though humanlike robots are still fairly primitive, it's (2) ______________ that "in five or ten years androids will routinely be functioning in human environments," says Reid Simmons, a professor of robotics at Carnegie Mellon University. These versatile and (3) ______________ machines will cook for us, wash and fold the laundry, and even care for and teach our children while we watch from a computer miles away. Though such technology now seems innovative, by 2100, say scientists, we'll (4) ______________ it ______________, just like we do driving a car or making a phone call. Other ways that robots might transform our lives:

- Robotic autocars will drive for us, which will make the roads safer.
- Microscopic medical "nanobots" will repair old cells and cure diseases, increasing our lives by hundreds of years.
- Flying drones will deliver packages and pizzas right to our doors, making delivery people (5) ______________.

This drone has a camera and can be used by police.

C Do you think that using robots will make our lives better? Why or why not? What might be some of the positive and negative consequences? Discuss your answers with a partner.

Grammar

A Study the chart and answer the questions below with a partner.

Predictions with Future Forms	
future continuous: Use to show that an event will be ongoing in the future.	*will/be going to* + *be* + present participle ❶ In five or ten years, robots **will be functioning** in human environments.
future perfect: Use to show that a future event will be finished by some future point in time.	*will* + *have* + past participle ❷ By 2020, scientists believe that we **will have found** a cure for certain types of cancer.
future in the past: Use to talk in present time about a prediction that was made in the past.	*would* or *was/were going to* + base form of the verb Carlos thought getting a job after graduation **would be** hard, but he was hired by a company right away.

❶ It would also be correct to use the simple future or *be going to* here. Notice though that the simple future states that an action will or won't happen. The future continuous emphasizes the duration or ongoing status of the action.
❷ This sentence means that at some point before 2020, scientists will discover a cure for cancer. It would also be possible to say here, *We will find a cure for cancer by 2020*.

Which form do we use to talk about . . .

- an ongoing event in the future?
- a prediction that was made previously?
- an event that will be finished at some point in the future?

B Complete the sentences using the correct future form of the verb in parentheses. Sometimes more than one answer is possible. Check your answers with a partner.

1. Over the next decade, more women (enter) ____________ the workplace, and many more companies (hire) ____________ female managers and CEOs.
2. By the end of the twenty-first century, experts believe we (exhaust) ____________ all major oil reserves.
3. In 1900, an American magazine predicted that Russian (be) ____________ the second most widely-spoken language in the world after English.
4. Experts believe almost 70% of the world's people (live) ____________ in cities by 2050.
5. *Futurist Magazine* predicts that by 2021, commercial space travel (become) ____________ very popular and that more than thirteen thousand people (travel) ____________ into space.
6. In the late 1960s, artist Andy Warhol said that one day, everyone (have) ____________ a chance to be famous for fifteen minutes. Thanks to the Internet, his prediction has come true.

C Make your own prediction about society, fashion, travel, education, work, or another topic, and write it on the board. Then read your classmates' ideas. Which predictions seem feasible? Which don't? Why? Tell a partner.

Ask Answer Look at the past predictions in Exercise **B**. Can you think of any other predictions that people made in the past that did or didn't come true?

Listening

A At a recent press conference, an aviation expert answered questions about the future of air travel. Read the questions below. Do you think the expert will answer *yes* or *no*? Why? Tell a partner.

______ Will we someday commute to work in flying cars?

______ In the future, will commerical airliners fly faster than they do now?

______ Is it possible that we'll ever use jet packs to get around?

B Which question is the expert answering? Listen and write the correct number (1, 2, or 3) next to each question in Exercise **A**.

C How did the expert actually respond to each question? Read the Listening Strategy. Then listen again and circle *yes* or *no*. Fill in the notes on the reasons he gives for each response.

Man in flight using a jet pack

Listening Strategy **Signal Phrases** As you listen, pay attention to how the speaker uses these signal phrases to explain his reasons: *For a couple of reasons . . .; One of the main reasons is . . .; There are good reasons why . . .; Keep in mind, too, that . . .; Another important reason is that . . .* When you hear these used, be prepared to take notes on what the speaker says. As you're taking notes, try to list only key words (nouns, verbs, adjectives, numbers), not every word.

Question	Response	Reasons
1	yes / no	a. The cost of __________: the more you use, the more __________ a flight is. b. Traveling at __________ speeds isn't __________; the plane can __________ in the air.
2	yes / no	a. An accident would almost always be __________. b. Most models that we have now aren't __________. You can't switch from __________ to __________.
3	yes / no	a. ______________________________ b. ______________________________

D Look back at the reasons you wrote in Exercise **C** and answer the following questions about the expert's comments with a partner.

1. Which forms of air transportation did people in the past predict we'd have by now?
2. Which one does the expert believe we'll be using in the future? What are some of the current challenges of using this form of transportation?
3. Were you surprised by any of the expert's answers? Why or why not?

Connections

Scientists prepare an experiment using fiber optic cables.

A Read the predictions below about the workplace. Then answer Questions 1–3 with a partner. When you're done, list your ideas to Questions 2 and 3 on the board.

1. Which items are already common where you live?
2. Can you think of other skills that people will need in the future?
3. What are some things you can do to get the skills needed to succeed in the workplace?

Today's Workplace . . . and Tomorrow's

- People will be changing jobs more often. Fewer people will be staying with one company in the same position for life. Many more people will be freelancing or starting their own businesses.
- People will need to be versatile and efficient—not just good at one thing, but skilled in many different areas.
- Innovative critical thinkers with problem-solving skills will be in demand.
- The ability to interact effectively with others will continue to be in demand, as many more people will be expected to work in teams to get jobs done.
- Those who are fluent in English and at least one other language will be favored over monolingual speakers.
- Your prediction: ______________________________

B On your own, write your answers to the questions below on a separate piece of paper.

1. What is your current occupation? If you are a student, what are you studying?
2. What are some of your short- and long-term career goals? For example, what do you expect you'll be doing a year from now? How about five years from now?
3. How do you plan to accomplish those goals?
4. Do you feel that you have the skills necessary to be successful in tomorrow's workplace? Why or why not? If not, what are you planning to do to improve your skill set?

C Get together with a partner and take turns asking and answering the questions in Exercise **B**. What do you think of your partner's plans? What other suggestions can you give?

What are some of your short- and long-term career goals?

A year from now, I'll be applying to graduate school. Five years from now, I will have taken my company public.

D Repeat Exercise **C** with two other partners. Then share the most helpful piece of advice you got with the rest of the class.

Reading

atmosphere layer of air or gas around a planet
habitable good enough for people to live in

Did you know?

Earth's atmosphere . . .

- provides us with the oxygen we need to breathe.
- protects us from the sun's harmful rays.
- keeps our planet warm enough for plants to grow and for oceans, rivers, and seas to form.

A How much do you know about the planet Mars? Work with a partner and mark each statement *True* or *False*. Use your dictionary to help you understand the words in bold.

1. Scientists believe there was once a lot of water on the surface of Mars. That water is now **frozen** in the planet's **polar** regions.
2. Mars isn't a habitable planet for humans. It's too cold, and it has a very **thin** atmosphere.
3. There is less **gravity** on Mars than there is on Earth.
4. Mars is often called the "red planet" because its **soil** is red.

B Read the article's title and subtitle, and look at the image on page 67. How would you answer the questions in the subtitle? Discuss your ideas with a partner. Then read the article to check your ideas.

C How might humans transform Mars into a habitable planet? Match a time from the Thousand-Year Project with an event.

a. Every eighteen months
b. In the first one hundred years
c. By the year 200
d. By the year 600
e. By the year 1,000

1. ______ humans will be able to grow trees and other plants.
2. ______ humans will have started living in cities.
3. ______ an atmosphere starts to form as humans release CO_2 into the air.
4. ______ humans will travel to Mars; each new group will set up new buildings.
5. ______ water will have begun to flow and Mars's surface will have started to change.

Exploration on Mars

D Robert Zubrin gives two reasons for transforming Mars into a habitable planet. On a separate piece of paper, list the reasons and their benefits. Then compare answers with a partner.

Ask Answer Do you think making Mars the new Earth is really feasible? Is it a good idea? Why or why not?

Making Mars the New Earth

What would it take to green[1] the red planet, and should we do it?

Could we transform Mars's frozen surface into something more friendly and Earthlike? And if we could, the question is: Should we? The first question has a clear answer: Yes, we probably could. Spacecraft exploring Mars have found evidence that the planet was warm in its youth and had rivers and large seas. Scientists believe that we could return Mars to this state by adding greenhouse gases like carbon dioxide into the planet's air. This would help create an atmosphere, which in turn would warm the planet, melt polar ice, and allow water to flow.

Transforming Mars into a habitable planet for humans could take centuries, but many supporters of the idea believe the effort would be worth it. Aerospace engineer Robert Zubrin, for example, believes that there are at least two good reasons to do it. The first is that going to Mars will challenge us, especially our youth. From this project, we could get millions of new scientists, doctors, inventors, and engineers. Zubrin also believes that if we open Mars to humanity, we will have a place for our species to grow and evolve, which will help to ensure humans' long-term survival. Zubrin anticipates that years from now there will be hundreds of colonies on Mars. Because the gravity of Mars is less than on Earth, humans living there would eventually become lighter, taller, and slimmer. Earth people, by comparison, would appear a bit short and heavy. What we would have, says Zubrin, is species divergence.[2] In biology, he explains, a species is considered successful if it has many different types. Socially and culturally, humans would also evolve. Zubrin says Mars will be settled by different groups of people who want to live where the rules haven't been created yet. As a result, the inhabitants of Mars will likely develop a new way of life with unique languages, customs, literature, and technology.

Ultimately, manned missions to Mars would not only benefit people here on Earth, but also help to ensure humans' long-term survival. And for these reasons, say Zubrin and others, the journey and the expense would be worth it.

[1] **green** to make habitable for plant and animal life
[2] **divergence** separating; drawing apart

The THOUSAND-YEAR Project

Year 0: The project begins with a series of eighteen-month survey missions. Each crew making the six-month journey to Mars adds new housing and other buildings to the site.

Year 100: An atmosphere starts to form as humans add greenhouse gases like CO_2 into the planet's air.

Year 200: The temperature of the planet is now warmer. Rain starts to fall and water begins to flow. Mars's red soil begins to green very slightly.

Year 600: Small rivers and lakes have formed. There is now enough oxygen in the soil and atmosphere to grow flowers and plants.

Year 1,000: There are now a number of human colonies on Mars. Some people are living in cities. Though the planet is now warmer and greener, humans can still only go outside wearing breathing equipment. It will be thousands of years before there is enough oxygen outside for humans to move around without breathing equipment.

Writing

Make a Counterargument

A Read the first two paragraphs of this essay and then discuss Questions 1–3 with a partner.

Robert Zubrin feels that sending humans to Mars to transform it into a habitable planet is a good idea. Though he has some good reasons why we should do it, the disadvantages outweigh the benefits for three main reasons.

The first drawback is the enormous risk and uncertainty of the project. Zubrin says that going to Mars will challenge us and help us produce millions of skilled workers. **However**, it's difficult to justify spending lots of money on a project where the chances of success are so uncertain. We know very little about living on Mars. Failure is actually quite feasible. If the mission is not successful, those millions of jobs will not come as expected. To truly challenge ourselves, we should start by using the money to research real problems we face right here on Earth, such as cancer or poverty.

1. Is the writer agreeing with or disagreeing with Robert Zubrin?
2. What reason does the writer give for her opinion?
3. Do you think she makes a good argument against Zubrin? Why or why not?

B Zubrin gives two more reasons why we should develop colonies on Mars. You want to argue against his ideas. Read items 2 and 3 below. Then match a drawback from the box with each of Zubrin's reasons or think of your own. Explain your reasons to a partner.

1. It will produce millions of new scientists, doctors, etc.
   Drawback: the risk and uncertainty
2. It will ensure humans' long-term survival.
   Drawback: ______________________
3. Humans will have the opportunity to create a new world with new rules.
   Drawback: ______________________

Possible Drawbacks

- We have problems to deal with on Earth first.
- Living in a place with no laws could be dangerous.
- Humans on Mars would face serious health risks.
- other: ______________________

C Write two more paragraphs for the essay in Exercise **A** on a separate piece of paper. Base these paragraphs on the drawbacks you listed in Exercise **B**.

1. First, read the Writing Strategy. Then for each paragraph, outline your ideas by doing the following: (1) state the drawback (*The second drawback is. . .*); (2) state Zubrin's point (*Zubrin says going to Mars will ensure. . .*); (3) offer your counterargument and clearly explain your reason (*However, . . .*).
2. Use your outline to write paragraphs 3 and 4.

Writing Strategy

Making a Counterargument

A counterargument, or rebuttal, argues against someone else's opinion, either because it is incorrect or because you have another point of view. A counterargument states:

- The opinion you disagree with: *Zubrin says that going to Mars will challenge us and help us produce millions of skilled workers.*
- Your opinion and reason for disagreeing: *However, it's difficult to justify spending lots of money on a project where the chances of success are so uncertain.*

Note that a rebuttal is often introduced using words like *however, yet,* and *that said.*

D Exchange papers with a partner, and read his or her paragraphs. Do you think your partner makes good counterarguments against Zubrin? Why or why not?

Speaking

A Read the questions below and think about your answers. You will need to support each of your responses with reasons and/or examples. Take some notes on a separate piece of paper.

1. In general, do you think space exploration is useful? Why or why not? Explain your answer.
2. Many people have said that given the chance, they would volunteer for a one-way journey to Mars to colonize the planet. If you were given that opportunity, would you do it? Why?
3. Every year, scientists discover more planets. Some say that it's feasible that by 2100 we will have made contact with other life forms. Does this make you feel hopeful or worried? Why?

B Work with a partner. Take turns answering the questions using your notes. You will have twenty minutes total. Continue until you have both answered each of the questions or time is up.

1. **Student A:** Choose one question (1–3) from Exercise **A** and answer it. Talk for one minute.
   Student B: When your partner is finished, answer these questions and share your feedback with Student A:
   - Did Student A keep talking without stopping or hesitating a lot?
   - Did Student A explain his or her ideas in detail and make sense when he/she talked?
2. Switch roles and repeat steps 1 and 2 until all questions are answered.

C Share your answers with the class. Which were the most common? Do the results surprise you?

Video

inspire to encourage or make someone want to do something

Johan Reinhard

A Read the information about three National Geographic explorers. Have you ever heard of these people? What do these three explorers have in common? Tell a partner.

ALEXANDRA COUSTEAU

Environmental advocate (and granddaughter of Jacques Cousteau) who raises awareness about global water issues and inspires people to protect the planet's waters

JOHAN REINHARD

Anthropologist who has done extensive field research in the Andes and Himalayas investigating the cultural practices of mountain people

SYLVIA EARLE

Oceanographer who has led numerous underwater expeditions around the world, researching marine ecosystems and advocating for the environment

B Read these questions. Next, watch the video of Alexandra Cousteau and write the numbers (1–2) of the questions she answers. Then watch the video of Johan Reinhard and Sylvia Earle and do the same.

1. When you were young, what inspired your interest in exploration?
2. What is the most exciting part of your job?

(Segment 1): Alexandra Cousteau ________________ **(Segment 2):** Johan Reinhard ________________

(Segment 3): Sylvia Earle ________________

C Read the excerpts from the video below. Then watch the video again and paraphrase each underlined word or expression with a partner. Write on a separate piece of paper and use your dictionary to help you.

1. **Cousteau:** Every new place is always a revelation.
2. **Reinhard:** Probably the things that most excited me for discoveries weren't so much the mummies per se, but . . .
3. **Earle:** It's finding, not just new things, but new ideas to begin to connect the dots.

Sylvia Earle

D Join another pair and choose one side of the following question: *Which kind of exploration is more important: ocean exploration or archeological exploration?* Pairs should not choose the same side of the debate. Carefully plan your argument and then debate your position against the other pair.

Expanding Your Fluency

It is the year 2200. You and your classmates are colonists on your way to Mars. Though humans have been going to Mars for several years, the life you'll lead will still be fairly primitive:

- You'll be living in a small house, which you will share with four other people. You'll be spending a lot of time inside, as it will only be about 32°F (0°C) outside during the day.
- You won't have running water, and personal electricity use will be limited to one hour a day. Entertainment that you took for granted on Earth (movies, music, games) won't exist on Mars.
- Once a year, you will receive food, clothing, and medical supplies from Earth, but for the most part, you will need to grow all of your own food and repair everything you own.

Other facts:

- There are already fifty other small colonies on the planet populated by adults and children. Some are friendly and open, while others are closed and hostile to outsiders.
- People speak different languages.
- Once a month, colonies trade goods and interact with each other at indoor marketplaces.

Read the information above. Then get into a group of five people and do the following:

1. Each person should choose a role: architect, environmentalist, interpreter, nurse, engineer android, or another role of your choosing. On your own, think about these questions:
   - What skills or talents do you bring to the group?
   - How will you be able to improve the quality of life for yourself and your fellow colonists?
   - What job(s) will you be able to do?
2. Explain your answers to your partners; they will ask you questions to learn more.
3. Once on Mars, your group discovers that you have only enough resources to support <u>four</u> colonists. Because of this, one of you must leave the colony. Each person in the group will have one minute to explain why he or she should stay and why the others should leave.
4. Which person would you vote out of the colony? State who you chose to "vote off" and explain your reasons. The person who receives the most votes must go.

Check What You Know

Rank how well you can perform these outcomes on a scale of 1–5 (5 being the best).

__________ make predictions using different future forms
__________ identify key words used to explain reasons
__________ describe skills needed to achieve future goals
__________ develop and write a counterargument

Pronunciation

Stress on Content Words versus Function Words

Most sentences contain content words and function words.

The **effects** of **so** many **languages disappearing** could be a **cultural disaster**.

Content words carry meaning and are usually stressed, that is, spoken more clearly and loudly. Content words usually include key nouns and pronouns, main verbs, adjectives, and adverbs.

Function words usually do not carry meaning and are usually unstressed, that is, spoken more quickly and can be harder to hear in everyday conversation. Function words include articles, auxiliary verbs, conjunctions, determiners, prepositions, and pronouns.

Listen to the sentence and notice the difference in stress on content and function words.

Alice was **beginning** to get **very tired** of **waiting** for the **bus** in the **rain**.

TIP Remember that words are not stressed simply because they are content words. Content words are stressed if they carry important meaning. Also, function words are sometimes stressed to draw the listener's attention to that particular word.

Practice

A Listen to the sentences. Mark the words that are stressed. How are they different than the unstressed words?

1. The baby slept well and is very happy today.
2. Cecilia enjoys surfing and rock climbing.
3. The doctor said that I have the flu.

B Identify the content words and function words in each sentence. Say the sentences with stress on the content words. Then listen and repeat to check your work.

1. The dogs are both wet from the rain.
2. Who went with you to the movies last night?
3. Natalie said that Ms. Norton is her favorite teacher.
4. I need to write a few more sentences to finish my essay.
5. That was the most beautiful sunset I've ever seen.
6. You must have run quickly to get here on time.
7. I've never eaten at that restaurant before.
8. Where did you learn to speak Portuguese?
9. My sister just gave birth to twin boys.
10. I'll have soup and salad.

Differences between American English and British English

Playwright George Bernard Shaw said that America and Great Britain are "two countries separated by a common language." The Americans and the British both speak English, of course, but there are some differences in grammar, word choice, spelling, and especially pronunciation. Below are some examples of the pronunciation differences.

Pronunciation			
Differences	**Examples**	**American**	**British**
letter *a*	ask, grass	/æsk/, /græs/	/ask/, /gras/
letter *r*	forty, board	/fɔrti/, /bɔrd/	/fɔti/, /bɔd/
intrusive /r/	idea of, saw a	/aidiə əv/, /sɔ ə/	/aidiər əv/, /sɔr ə/
-ery, *-ary*	cemetery, ordinary	/sɛmətɛri/, /ɔrdənɛri/	/sɛmətri/, /ɔrdɪnəri/

The intrusive *r* sound occurs in British English between a word ending in vowel sounds such as /ə/ and /ɔ/ and another word beginning with a vowel sound. In British English there is also a tendency to omit or reduce the vowel sound in the word endings *-ery* and *-ary*, producing /ri/ or /əri/ instead of /ɛri/.

There are also some differences in spelling patterns between British and American English. Note that these differences do not affect pronunciation.

Spelling

-or (Am) vs. -our (Br)	-ize (Am) vs. -ise (Br)	-er (Am) vs. -re (Br)
color/colour	recognize/recognise	center/centre
flavor/flavour	organization/organisation	meter/metre

Practice

A Listen to the two pronunciations of the words below. For each one, choose *Am* if the pronunciation is American English or *Br* if the pronunciation is British English. Check your answers. Then listen again and repeat.

1.	a. staff	Am / Br	b. staff	Am / Br
2.	a. short	Am / Br	b. short	Am / Br
3.	a. military	Am / Br	b. military	Am / Br
4.	a. agenda is	Am / Br	b. agenda is	Am / Br
5.	a. banana	Am / Br	b. banana	Am / Br
6.	a. record	Am / Br	b. record	Am / Br
7.	a. extraordinary	Am / Br	b. extraordinary	Am / Br
8.	a. stationery	Am / Br	b. stationery	Am / Br
9.	a. thawing	Am / Br	b. thawing	Am / Br
10.	a. secretary	Am / Br	b. secretary	Am / Br

Reducing to Schwa: *to*

Reduction occurs in spoken language when sounds are shortened and/or changed slightly. In English, the vowel sound in the word *to* is often reduced from /oʊ/ to schwa /ə/. For example:

- Elias covered his head with a towel to keep cool.
- My class ends at a quarter to two.

Often, this reduction occurs when *to* appears before the words *him* or *her*.

- I need to speak to him in the morning.
- The letter was addressed to her, not you.

This reduction also occurs when *to* is paired with other words, for example *ought*, *have*, and *going*.

- There ought to be a law against that.
- I would go to the party, but I have to do homework.
- She told me that she's going to start college in the fall.

Notice that in some of these cases, the /t/ sound in *to* disappears and the sounds in the other words also change.

> **TIP** Do not reduce the vowel sound in *to* to schwa when it comes before another schwa, for example:
> - He's going to give his furniture to a friend.

Practice

A **Say each sentence aloud and then listen to the recording. Say the sentences again and then mark reductions of *to* in the sentences.**

1. I was going to call Jim, but I forgot.
2. Why did you give my MP3 player to her?
3. Let's move to another table.
4. Ava has to get good grades to go on the trip.
5. That book is overdue, and I really need to return it.
6. We ought to report the accident right now.
7. Do you think we can get them to agree on a meeting place?
8. Gavin sent a birthday present to a friend today.
9. You don't have to drive very far to your office.

Intonation to Show Sarcasm and Irony

Sarcasm is the use of **irony**, the opposite of what is actually meant, to be humorous or maybe even insulting. In spoken English, sarcasm is largely expressed by the way the words in a statement or question are said.

Listen to the sentences below. You will hear them read twice. The first time the intonation shows sincerity; the second time it shows sarcasm. Listen for the differences.

- He did a **great** job fixing your bike, **didn't he**?
- He did a **great** job fixing your bike, **didn't he**?

- That party was **so** much fun; I **can't wait** for the next one!
- That party was **so** much fun; I **can't wait** for the next one!

TIP Remember that these are general tendencies that speakers follow when being sarcastic. There are no set pronunciation rules.

For more on tag questions see pages 135 and 150.

In the first example, notice how an overemphasis on the words *great* and *didn't he* stand out in the sarcastic sentence; the speaker does not think he did a great job fixing the bike. Likewise, the words *so* and *can't wait* are overemphasized in the second; the speaker did not have fun at the party and is not looking forward to the next one. That strong, expected emphasis on key words indicates that the speaker actually means the opposite of the literal meaning of what they are saying.

Practice

A Listen to the pairs of sentences. Choose *sincere* or *sarcastic* for each sentence based on the intonation.

1. This sure is great weather we're having! **sincere / sarcastic**
2. This sure is great weather we're having! **sincere / sarcastic**
3. Yeah, this is exactly like you said it'd be. **sincere / sarcastic**
4. Yeah, this is exactly like you said it'd be. **sincere / sarcastic**
5. Do you think you could say that a little louder this time? **sincere / sarcastic**
6. Do you think you could say that a little louder this time? **sincere / sarcastic**
7. Take as much time as you like. **sincere / sarcastic**
8. Take as much time as you like. **sincere / sarcastic**
9. This line is moving really quickly. **sincere / sarcastic**
10. This line is moving really quickly. **sincere / sarcastic**
11. It's such a surprise to see you here. **sincere / sarcastic**
12. It's such a surprise to see you here. **sincere / sarcastic**
13. She's already so popular, isn't she? **sincere / sarcastic**
14. She's already so popular, isn't she? **sincere / sarcastic**

B Practice saying the sentences with your partner. Focus on using intonation to be either sincere or sarcastic. See if your partner can guess which one.

Reducing to Schwa: High-Frequency Function Words

As you already know, **reduction** occurs in spoken language when sounds are shortened and sometimes changed. **Function words** carry very little meaning, but have a grammatical role in the sentence. The vowel sounds in function words are frequently reduced to schwa in English.

Moira <u>can</u> help you with that.
The only model we have left is orange <u>and</u> green.
The dogs <u>will</u> run away if you leave the door open.
I told <u>you</u> I was going to win.
<u>Do</u> we know how many people are coming?

Practice

A **Say each sentence and then listen to the recording. Circle the function words that have been reduced to schwa. Listen again and check your answers.**

1. Be sure to pack a suit and tie for the trip.
2. Colin doesn't know when we can leave.
3. Hard times will have that effect on people.
4. The chef forgot to put salt and pepper in the dish.
5. How do I reach the manager?
6. He refused to tell you the secret, didn't he?
7. What are you doing for dinner?
8. My sister can give them a discount.
9. Everyone will need a paper and pencil.
10. They can speak French and German.

The Prominence of Stress

In speech, you can stress different words to modify the meaning of what you say. The same sentence said in different ways can have a slightly different meaning depending on the specific words that are emphasized; this use of stress clarifies the exact meaning of the sentence to the listener.

Take the sentence *Artists often make sacrifices for their work*. Read three different ways, this sentence has slightly different meanings. Listen to it read three times and pay attention to how the stressed word in each example makes the exact meaning more precise in each case.

- **Artists** often make sacrifices for their work.
  (One type of person that might have to make sacrifices to pursue their work is artists.)
- Artists **often** make sacrifices for their work.
  (Artists don't occasionally make sacrifices for their work; they do it all the time.)
- Artists often make **sacrifices** for their work.
  (Often, artists don't make a lot of money for their work; their commitment to their art takes personal sacrifice.)

Practice

A Listen to the sentences and circle the stressed word in each sentence. Then choose the emphasized meaning based on the word stress.

1. Sherry took a picture of Ben and his dog.
   a. Sherry's action was "took."
   b. Sherry took the picture, and not someone else.
   c. Sherry took a picture, and not something else.
2. Sherry took a picture of Ben and his dog.
   a. The picture also showed Ben's dog.
   b. The dog belongs to Ben.
   c. Sherry's picture also showed Ben.
3. I put two magazines in the desk drawer.
   a. There are going to be more magazines.
   b. The magazines belong to me.
   c. There are two magazines only.
4. I put two magazines in the desk drawer.
   a. The magazines' location is a drawer.
   b. I didn't do anything besides put the magazines in the drawer.
   c. The magazines are inside a drawer in a specific piece of furniture.
5. Yesterday he rode the bus to school.
   a. The bus only came yesterday.
   b. The day was yesterday, not any other.
   c. He didn't drive; he rode the bus.
6. Yesterday he rode the bus to school.
   a. The school was his destination.
   b. He rides the bus to work sometimes.
   c. The school is near the bus stop.
7. My daughter drew that beautiful picture on the refrigerator.
   a. I'm talking about my daughter's picture, not another picture.
   b. I'm talking about my daughter, not my son.
   c. I'm talking about my daughter, not other people's daughters.
8. My daughter drew that beautiful picture on the refrigerator.
   a. I think the picture is gorgeous.
   b. The picture is that one, not others.
   c. The picture is on the refrigerator, not on the wall.
9. The flight normally leaves at 7:30 in the morning.
   a. The flight leaves at 7:30, not sooner.
   b. The flight is a morning flight.
   c. The morning is the usual time the flight leaves.
10. The flight normally leaves at 7:30 in the morning.
   a. The flight usually leaves at this time, but sometimes it's late.
   b. The plane leaves, not the bus.
   c. The flight departs at 7:30; it does not arrive.

Intonation in Tag Questions

A **tag question** consists of a statement and a question structure added to the end of the statement. The statement portion of the tag question normally uses falling intonation. The tag can use either rising or falling intonation depending on the speaker's meaning.

- **Rising intonation** in the tag indicates that the speaker thinks the statement is true, but he or she isn't certain. In other words, the speaker is asking a real question.
- **Falling intonation** in the tag indicates stronger certainty in the truth of the statement. The speaker is not asking a true question so much as anticipating agreement.

Below are two sentences that use **rising intonation** in the tag. Listen carefully to the intonation in each example. Note that it rises on the tag because the speaker is truly seeking an answer.

- That was your sister, wasn't it?
- You didn't eat the last piece of cake, did you?

Below are the same two sentences, but with falling intonation in the tag. Listen carefully to the intonation in each example. Note that it falls on the tag because the speaker is anticipating agreement.

- That was your sister, wasn't it?
- You didn't eat the last piece of cake, did you?

Practice

A **Listen to the recording and then repeat the sentences. Then decide if the speaker is asking a true question or anticipating agreement. When you are done, check answers with a partner. Then take turns asking the questions.**

1. You're Adele's cousin, aren't you? **question / agreement**
2. That's the same jacket as mine, isn't it? **question / agreement**
3. There are over a dozen people in the group, aren't there? **question / agreement**
4. They shouldn't have told him, should they? **question / agreement**
5. You remembered to reschedule the meeting, didn't you? **question / agreement**
6. He's got a unique sense of humor, doesn't he? **question / agreement**
7. You went to the party last night, didn't you? **question / agreement**
8. Eating bananas makes you sleepy, doesn't it? **question / agreement**
9. They were both born in November, weren't they? **question / agreement**
10. You brought the present, didn't you? **question / agreement**

B **Write two tag questions: one that asks for an actual answer and another that expects agreement. Read your questions to a partner using the correct intonation. Then ask your partner which type of tag question it is.**

1. ______________________________
2. ______________________________

Language Summary

Unit 1

adapt to change ideas or behavior in order to deal with something successfully **adaptable** (adj.)
clarify to explain something in order to make it easier to understand **clarification** (n.) **clarity** (n.)
collaborative done by two or more people working together **to collaborate** (v.) **collaboration** (n.)
conflict a serious argument about something important
convey to express a thought or feeling so that it is understood **conveyance** (n.)
detect to find or discover that something is present **detector** (n.) **detectable** (adj.)
distinct noticeably separate or different **distinctly** (adv.) **distinctive** (adj.)
document to record the details of an event **document** (n.) **documentation** (n.)
ebb and flow come and go **to flow** (v.)
endure to continue to exist **endurance** (n.) **enduring** (adj.)
ensure to guarantee
factors something that affects an event, decision, or situation
impulsive doing and saying things suddenly without thinking about it carefully **impulsively** (adv.) **impulse** (n.)
knowledge information and understanding about a subject **knowledgeable** (adj.)
landline phone traditional or home phone
linguist a person who specializes in the study of languages **linguistics** (n.) **linguistic** (adj.)
possess to have or to own **possession** (n.) **possessive** (adj.)
preservation protection (for the future) **(to) preserve** (v., n.)
remark something that you say (fact or opinion) **to remark** (v.) **remarkable** (adj.)
sensitive showing an understanding of others' feelings **sensitivity** (n.) **insensitive** (adj.)
slave someone who is the property of another person **to enslave** (v.) **slavery** (n.)
switch to change
threatened endangered **to threaten** (v.) **threat** (n.)
vanish to disappear
whine to complain in an annoying way about something unimportant **whiney**, **whiny** (adj.)

Unit 2

affluent wealthy **affluence** (n.)
broke having no money
budget a plan that shows how much money you have and how much you can spend **to budget** (v.)
cheapskate a person that does not like to spend money
credit a method that allows you to buy things and pay for them later
debt money that you owe **debtor** (n.)
disposable income the extra money you have left over after all your bills are paid
economist a person who studies the way in which money is used in society **economy** (n.) **economic** (adj.)
entrepreneur a person who starts his or her own business **entrepreneurial** (adj.)
fair deal a good business arrangement
headache a big problem
impact to have an effect on someone or something **impact** (n.)
loan money you borrow or lend **to loan** (v.)
make ends meet to keep one's expenses within one's income
materialistic valuing money and possessions very highly **materialism** (n.)
my treat it's on me; to pay for another's food or entertainment
nest egg money that you save for a particular purpose
on the house without charge; free
pay back to return money that you owe someone
profit money that is earned in business minus expenses **nonprofit** (adj.) **profitable** (adj.)
run out (of something) to have no more of something
sacrifice to give up something valuable to help yourself or others **sacrifice** (n.)
save up (for something) to put aside money for future use **savings** (n.)
snowball to increase rapidly
splurge to spend a lot of money on something, usually something you don't need
stability a situation that is calm and not likely to change suddenly **stable** (adj.) **unstable** (adj.)
terms the parts of the contract that all sides must agree on (e.g., how much a loan is for, how long one has to pay it back, etc.)
thrifty careful with money
value to attach importance to something **to undervalue** (v.) **value** (n.) **valuable** (adj.)

Unit 3

ban to refuse to allow **ban** (n.)
chaotic in a state of complete disorder **chaos** (n.)
community a group of people that live in a particular place **communal** (adj.)
cosmopolitan full of people from many different countries
dense containing a lot of people or things in a small area; crowded **densely** (adv.) **density** (n.)
descendants people of later generations
destruction the state of being destroyed **to destroy** (v.) **destructive** (adj.)

district an area of a town or country
drought a long period of time in which no rain falls
dynamic full of energy
global affecting all parts of the world; international **globally** (adv.)
immigrant a person who moves permanently to a different country **to immigrate** (v.) **immigration** (n.)
in isolation (from) separately (from) **to isolate** (v.), **isolated** (adj.)
infrastructure the basic facilities (such as transportation, power supplies, and buildings) that allow a city or organization to function
inhabitant person who lives in a particular place **habitable** (adj.) **uninhabitable** (adj.)
livable suitable for living in
manageable able to be dealt with easily **to manage** (v.) **unmanageable** (adj.)
metropolitan relating to a large, busy city **metropolis** (n.)
nutrition the foods that you take into your body (and how they influence your health) **malnutrition** (n.) **nutritious** (adj.)
per capita (the amount) per person
rapid fast **rapidly** (adv.)
renewal the act of restoring **to renew** (v.)
soil the substance on the surface of the earth in which plants grow; dirt
stunt to prevent something from growing as much as it should **stunted** (adj.)
transformation a complete change in the appearance of something (usually for the better) **to transform** (v.) **transformative** (adj.)
urbanization the process by which more and more people move from rural areas to the cities **suburban** (adj.) **urban** (adj.)

Unit 4

affectionate loving and warm **affectionately** (adv.) **affection** (n.)
ambitious very motivated to succeed **ambition** (n.)
be hard on (someone) to treat someone in a severe or unkind way
bully using one's strength or power to hurt or frighten others **bully** (n.)
correlate to have a close connection to something else **correlation** (n.)
demanding difficult; insisting that something be done your way **to demand** (v.)
get along (with someone) to have a friendly relationship with someone else
idealistic hopeful; believing in the best **idealism** (n.)
innovative creative; original; inventive; new **to innovate** (v.) **innovator** (n.)
lab partner in a science class like biology or chemistry the student you work with in the laboratory to do certain experiments or exercises **laboratory** (n.)
longevity long life
obesity the state of being very overweight **obese** (adj.)
picky critical; hard to please; choosy
pushover a person who is easily influenced by others **to push around** (v.)
reserved keeping one's own feelings hidden
safety net money you can rely on if you get into a difficult financial situation
sedentary inactive; sitting a lot
sensible logical; realistic **commonsense** (n.) **nonsense** (n.)
stubborn inflexible; unwilling to change your mind **stubbornly** (adv.) **stubbornness** (n.)
supportive helpful and kind to those in need **(to) support** (v., n.)
tax incentive a decrease in the amount of tax one must pay, which allows one to do something else **incentivize** (v.)
thorough careful; detailed **thoroughly** (adv.) **thoroughness** (n.)
tolerant accepting and open-minded **to tolerate** (v.) **tolerance** (n.)
unplug to relax and do nothing
upbeat positive and cheerful **downbeat** (adj.)
wear the pants to be in control or the main decision maker (used to describe a person)
work (something) out to find a solution to a problem
zeal a strong enthusiasm for something **zealously** (adv.) **zealot** (n.)

Unit 5

absorb to reduce the force of something; soak up or take in **absorption** (n.) **absorbent** (adj.)
aggressive acting in an angry or violent manner **aggressively** (adv.) **aggression** (n.)
amber a hard yellowish-brown substance used to make jewelry **amber** (adj.)
archaeologist a person who studies people and societies of the past by examining their culture, architecture, tools, and other objects **archaeology** (n.)
Bronze Age the period of ancient human culture between 4000 and 1200 BCE
bury to place something in a hole in the ground and cover it with dirt **burial** (n.)
case a situation or incident
cemetery a place where the bodies or ashes of the dead are buried
clue something that helps you find the answer to a problem **clueless** (adj.)
complex a group of buildings designed for a particular purpose

Language Summary

exotic very different or unusual
geological related to the study of the Earth's rocks, minerals, and surface **geology** (n.) **geologist** (n.)
infection a disease caused by germs or bacteria **to infect** (v.) **infectious** (adj.)
kudos public admiration or recognition received when doing something
loot to steal from shops and houses **loot** (n.) **looter** (n.)
monument a large structure, usually made of stone, built to remind people of something
mystery something that is difficult to understand or explain **mysteriously** (adv.) **mysterious** (adj.)
narrow down to limit or restrict **narrowly** (adv.) **narrow** (adj.)
observation the act of carefully watching someone or something **to observe** (v.)
oxygen a gas in the air that all humans, animals, and plants need to live
profile a set of data that shows the important characteristics of someone or something **to profile** (v.)
settlement a place where people gather to build homes and live **to settle** (v.) **settler** (n.)
skeleton the frame of bones supporting a human or animal body **skeletal** (adj.)
solve to find an answer to a problem or crime **to resolve** (v.) **unsolved** (adj.)
speculate to guess about something's nature or identity **speculation** (n.) **speculative** (adj.)
surroundings the immediate area around you **to surround** (v.)
theory a formal idea that is intended to explain something **theoretically** (adv.) **theoretical** (adj.)
tow to pull something or someone by a rope tied to a vehicle
twist to turn **to untwist** (v.) **twisty** (adj.)
uncover to discover something previously unknown or hidden **to cover** (v.)
unharmed not hurt or damaged in any way **(to) harm** (v., n.) **harmful** (adj.)
withstand to survive or not give in to a force or action **to stand up to** (v.)

Unit 6

atmosphere layer of air or gas around a planet **atmospheric** (adj.)
cutting-edge the most advanced or most exciting in a particular field
divergence separating; drawing apart **to diverge** (v.) **divergent** (adj.)
drawback aspect of someone or something that makes them less acceptable
efficient able to do tasks successfully without wasting time or energy **efficiently** (adv.) **efficiency** (n.)
feasible possible **feasibility** (n.) **unfeasible** (adj.)
gravity the force that causes things to drop to the ground **gravitational** (adj.)
green to make habitable for plant and animal life **green** (adj.)
habitable good enough for people to live in **to inhabit** (v.) **uninhabitable** (adj.)
innovative creative; original; inventive; new **to innovate** (v.) **innovation** (n.)
inspire to encourage or make someone want to do something
interact (with) to communicate as you work or spend time together with others **interaction** (n.) **interactive** (adj.)
obsolete no longer necessary because something better has been invented
primitive simple; not well developed **primitively** (adv.)
revelation very surprising or very good **to reveal** (v.)
take (something) for granted to accept that something is true or normal without thinking about it
versatile able to be used for many different purposes **versatility** (n.)

Grammar Summary

Unit 1

	Quantifiers	
	General amounts	**Specific amounts (within a group)**
	Quantifiers describing general amounts are followed by plural count nouns and noncount nouns.	Quantifiers that describe specific amounts are followed by singular count nouns (except *both* and sometimes *each*).
large amount →	**All students** have cell phones.	All members of a group
	A lot of students call their parents after school.	**Each/Every student** has a cell phone.
	They spend **a lot of time** on their phones.	**Each of** ** the **students** has a cell phone.
	There are **many students** studying English.	**Any student** in this class can converse in English.
	Quite a few students speak English well.	
	Some students need help with their homework.	Talking about two things
	I have **some free time** and can help you.	The meeting will be on Monday or Tuesday.
	A few* students study other foreign languages.	**Both** days** are fine with me.
	We don't have **much time** to study for the exam.	**Either day** is fine.
nothing →	**None** of the **students** like homework.	**Neither day** works well for me.
	*Another common expression with *few* is *very few* (which is an even smaller amount).	****Each of** and **both** are followed by a plural count noun.

Much is not used alone in affirmative statements. Use *a lot of* instead: ~~*She has much time*~~. *She has a lot of time.*

Note that when *each* is the subject, the verb is singular. When *none* is the subject, the verb can be either singular or plural depending on the situation. For example:

> *None* (*not any*) *of the translators* ***speak*** *French.*
> *None* (*not one*) *of the translators* ***speaks*** *French.*

Unit 2

Noun Clauses	
noun clauses starting with *that*	I like this jacket. How much is it? I think **(that) it is $50**.
noun clauses starting with a *wh-* word	I like this jacket. How much is it? I don't know **how much it is**.

Some **noun clauses** begin with the word *that*.
Other **noun clauses** begin with a *wh-* word (*who, what, where, why, how, when, which, whose*). These clauses follow statement word order even though they start with a question word.

Certain verbs are commonly followed by a noun clause . . .

- verbs that describe an opinion, feeling, or mental state: *assume, believe, guess, forget, hope, know, remember, suppose, think, understand, wonder*
- verbs that describe something someone said: *admit, explain, mention, say, tell*

Notice! In everyday spoken English, sentences that use verbs such as ***assume***, ***believe***, ***guess***, ***hope***, ***suppose***, ***think*** can often be shortened using *so* instead of writing the full noun clause.

Q: *Can we afford a new laptop?*
A: *I think so.* (i.e., *I think that we can afford a new laptop.*)

Q: *Are you getting a good grade in this class?*
A: *I hope so!* (i.e., *I hope that I am getting a good grade in this class.*)

The negative form for *I guess/suppose/hope/think so,*would be:
I guess/suppose/hope not.
I don't think so.

Some noun clauses end with a period, and some end with a question mark. If you're making a statement, end with a period. If you're asking for feedback or suggestions, end with a question mark.

A noun clause is a dependent clause that acts like a noun in a sentence. For example, a noun clause can be used as a subject or an object of a verb.

I don't know ***why he borrowed so much money****.*
Why he borrowed so much money *is really confusing to me.*

Noun clauses can also follow adjectives.

I'm not ***sure*** *what to do.*

Unit 3

Notice! The form for the dynamic and stative passive is the same: a form of *be* + the past participle.

Dynamic and Stative Passive

Dynamic Passive	Stative Passive
Belize City, the former capital, **was** nearly **destroyed** by a hurricane in 1961. The government **was moved** to Belmopan in 1970.	Belmopan, the new capital, **is situated** inland on safer ground, but Belize City **is** still **known** as the financial and cultural center of the country.
• This form of the passive expresses an action. The focus is on the receiver of the action, not the performer. • Use *by* + agent to name the performer of the action. (We don't use a *by* phrase when the performer is unimportant, unknown, or is obvious.) • The past participle functions more like a verb than an adjective. It expresses the action.	• This form of the passive describes a state or condition. • Because there is no action being expressed, it's impossible to name the agent. • Instead, we use a form of the passive followed by a preposition (not necessarily *by*). • The past participle functions more like an adjective than a verb. It describes the subject.
Verbs used with dynamic passive: *built, created, destroyed, divided, moved, sent*	***Verbs used with stative passive:*** *acquaint (with), associate (with), cover (with), crowd (with), dress (in), involve (with), know (as), made (of), situate (on)*

Unit 4

Making Wishes

	Real Situation	Ideal Situation
❶ **about the present**	I'**m** kind of short.	I wish (that) I **were** taller.
	I **don't speak** French.	I wish (that) I **spoke** French.
	She **has to leave** the party now.	She wishes (that) she **didn't have to leave**.
❷ **about the past**	I **was** careless on the exam.	I wish (that) I **had been** more thorough!
❸ **with *would***	We can't hear the teacher.	We wish (that) the teacher **would speak** louder so we could hear him.

Use *wish* to . . .
❶ talk about something you would like. In the *that* clause, the verb is in a past form.
❷ express regret about something that happened. In the *that* clause, the verb is in the past perfect.
❸ express displeasure in the moment with something or someone and to say that you want it to change.

For *be*, use *were* with both singular and plural subjects. In everyday spoken English, *was* is also used.

The ideal situations can also be presented in a shortened form.

I'm not very outgoing, but I wish (*that*) *I were*. (I wish I were outgoing.)

I don't speak French fluently, but I wish (*that*) *I did*.(I wish I did speak French fluently.)

The difference between *wish* and *hope* can sometimes be confusing. When talking about a situation that is **present, hypothetical, but probably not possible**, use *wish*.

I wish (*that*) *I were rich*.

Note that the verb in the *that* clause takes a past form (were).

When talking about a **possible future** situation, use *hope*.

I hope (*that*) *I get into Stanford University!* (NOT: *I wish* (that) *I get into Stanford University*.)

Note that the verb in the *that* clause is often in the present tense.

Unit 5

Modals of Possibility in the Past, Present, and Future		
	Present/Future	**Past**
strong certainty	(9:45 a.m.) Joe's not here yet. He **must** be on his way, though.	(9:45 a.m.) Ann's not here yet. She **must have** left her house late.
weaker certainty	(9:50 a.m.) He's still not here. He **could/may/might** be stuck in traffic.	(9:50 a.m.) She's still not here. I **could have/may have/might have** told her the wrong time.
impossibility	(9:58 a.m.) He just got here. I **can't/ couldn't** be more relieved.	(the next day) Ann said she didn't see me at the zoo. She **couldn't have** looked very hard—I was there the whole time!

Unit 6

Predictions with Future Forms	
future continuous: Use to show that an event will be ongoing in the future.	*will/be going to* + *be* + present participle ❶ In five or ten years, robots **will be functioning** in human environments.
future perfect: Use to show that a future event will be finished by some future point in time.	*will* + *have* + past participle ❷ By 2020, scientists believe that we **will have found** a cure for certain types of cancer.
future in the past: Use to talk in present time about a prediction that was made in the past.	*would* or *was/were going to* + base form of the verb Carlos thought getting a job after graduation **would be** hard, but he was hired by a company right away.

❶ It would also be correct to use the simple future or *be going to* here. Notice though that the simple future states that an action will or won't happen. The future continuous emphasizes the duration or ongoing status of the action.

❷ This sentence means that at some point before 2020, scientists will discover a cure for cancer. It would also be possible to say here, *We will find a cure for cancer by 2020.*

Grammar Summary

Skills Index

2A

World Class

WORKBOOK

NANCY DOUGLAS | JAMES R. MORGAN

NATIONAL GEOGRAPHIC LEARNING | CENGAGE Learning®

Australia • Brazil • Japan • Korea • Mexico • Singapore • Spain • United Kingdom • United States

CONTENTS

Credits

Photo Credits

p. 4: Olinchuk/Shutterstock.com; **p. 8:** ©iStockphoto.com/Gencay M. Emin; **p. 9** top: ©iStockphoto.com/Viktor Pryymachuk, bottom: ©iStockphoto.com/Anna Zielińska; **p. 10** top: JeremyRichards/Shutterstock.com, bottom: Luba V. Nel/Shutterstock.com; **p.15:** Tyler Olson/Shutterstock.com; **p. 16** top: Songquan Deng/Shutterstock.com, bottom: littleny/Shutterstock.com; **p. 20:** ©iStockphoto.com/Jason Lawes; **p. 22:** ©iStockphoto.com/Tanuki Photography; **p. 24** top: Andresr/Shutterstock.com, bottom: Maree Stachel-Williamson/Shutterstock.com; **p. 27:** Jo Ann Snover/Shutterstock.com; **p. 29** left: ©iStockphoto.com/Arild Heitmann, right: ©iStockphoto.com/pius99; **p. 30** top: Amy Toensing/National Geographic Stock, bottom: ©iStockphoto.com/ollo; **p. 34:** Boris Pamikov/Shutterstock.com; **p. 36** top: catwalker/Shutterstock.com, bottom: Geminoid HI-1 was developed by Hiroshi Ishiguro Laboratory, Advanced Telecommunications Research Institute International (ATR). Geminoid is a registered trademark of Advanced Telecommunications Research Institute International (ATR).

Text Credits

Readings from the following units were adapted from National Geographic. **Unit 1** Adapted from *Chile Expedition*, National Geographic Magazine, January 2011. **Unit 2** Adapted from *The Real Price of Gold* by Brook Larmer, National Geographic Magazine, January 2009. **Unit 3** Adapted from *Urban Downtime* by Jennifer Ackerman, National Geographic Magazine, October 2006. **Unit 4** Adapted from *Stop Food Cravings Through Imaginary Eating?* by Christine Dell'Amore, National Geographic Magazine, December 2010. **Unit 5** Adapted from *Shipwreck in the Forbidden Zone* by Roff Smith, National Geographic Magazine, October 2009. **Unit 6** Adapted from *Us. And them.* by Chris Carroll and Max Aguilera-Hellweg, National Geographic Magazine, August 2011.

1 Language and Life

Vocabulary and Grammar

Unit 1 Outcomes

- use quantifiers to talk about amounts
- bring up negative and sensitive topics
- work with restatement questions
- interpret and question the results of a report summary

A Read the words in the box. Complete the sentences with the correct word and form. Some words are extra.

adapted	**knowledge**
clarify	**remark**
collaborative	**sensitive**
impulsive	**whine**

1. This exam tests your __________ of how to use quantifiers.
2. It's not too difficult, so I don't want to hear you __________ about it.
3. All of the material in the exam is __________ from your textbook.
4. Think about the questions carefully. Don't be __________ when you answer.
5. When you finish the exam, be __________ to students who are still working. Don't talk!
6. Read the directions carefully. Is there anything you want me to __________?

B Read Bianca's e-mail to her cousin. Circle the correct quantifier to complete the sentence.

Send Chat Attach Address Font Colors Save as Draft

To: Chiara

Subject: Hi!

This week I started classes at the bilingual school. It's exciting to hear conversations in (1) either / both languages! (2) Every / A lot of day I learn (3) so much / so many vocabulary. (4) Some / Every students speak English very well. (5) A few / None students lived in England for a while. That's why they know so (6) much / many vocabulary. My new classmates and I spend a lot of time speaking English. My English is improving (7) many / every day!

OUTCOME MET: use quantifiers to talk about amounts

C Answer the questions with complete sentences.

1. Do you like to work on **collaborative** projects with your classmates? Why or why not? ______________________
2. What would you say to someone who **whines**? ______________________
3. Do all people who are **sensitive** try to avoid **conflict**, or can some sensitive people **adapt** themselves to tense situations? ______________________

D Finish the sentences with your own ideas.

1. A lot of my friends ______________________
2. Most people I know ______________________

3. Every student in my class ____________________

4. None of my friends ____________________

5. When I have some free time ____________________

E Use the word prompts to write sentences according to your own experiences. Be sure to pay close attention to the use of quantifiers. You may change the order of the words in the prompt.

Example: some / knowledge *Most people have some knowledge of how to use a cell phone.*

1. both / possess ____________________
2. a lot of / whine ____________________
3. quite a few / sensitive ____________________
4. every / adapt ____________________
5. many / remark ____________________
6. a few / conflict ____________________

OUTCOME MET: use quantifiers to talk about amounts

Video

A Watch the video and check (✓) *True* or *False*. Then correct the false sentences.

	True	False
1. There are nearly six thousand living languages known to scientists.	☐	☐
2. The Enduring Voices team recorded the stories and vocabulary of the Koro speakers.	☐	☐
3. The Koro language reflects a lot of knowledge about plant, animal, and human life in that valley.	☐	☐
4. That knowledge exists in other Tibeto-Burman languages, too.	☐	☐
5. Slaves may have been the first Koro speakers.	☐	☐

B Do you think Koro is an endangered language? Explain your answer.

Writing

A Read the summary of a report about disappearing languages. Then answer the questions below.

Overview: Today there are approximately six thousand languages spoken in the world. Half of those languages may disappear over the next one hundred years. The Enduring Voices team wants to reverse this trend. The Enduring Voices Project identifies endangered languages in order to save them from being lost.

Why every language matters

- every language is unique
- language is an important part of culture
- oral languages will be lost if they are not documented

Why languages die out

- languages of powerful groups become dominant
- official policies often require people to learn and speak the dominant language
- parents do not speak the ancestral language with their children

How Enduring Voices preserves languages

- record the sounds of the spoken language
- document the language in books and dictionaries
- record the stories, songs, and oral histories
- teach it to the younger generations

1. What is the purpose of the report? ______________________________
____
2. What are the three main points of the report? ______________________________
____
3. Did any of the information surprise you? Why or why not? ______________________________
____

B Think of three questions you would ask the Enduring Voices team about the report.

Example: *How do you write an oral language?*

1. ______________________________
2. ______________________________
3. ______________________________

C Use the information in the report to explain the work of Enduring Voices and why it is important. Include questions that the report raises in your mind.

____
____
____
____
____
____
____
____

OUTCOME MET: interpret and question the results of a report summary

Reading

The Dying Huilliche Languages of Chile

The Enduring Voices team went to the south central region of Chile to learn about the endangered South American language, Huilliche. They learned that there are actually two distinct languages spoken by the Huilliche community, and that both are more endangered than previously thought.

The Huilliche community includes the Choroy Traiguen people who live on the coast of the Osorno Province and the Wequetrumao who live on the island of Chiloe. The Choroy Traiguen speak *Tsesungun*, and the Wequetrumao speak *Huillichesungun*. The two languages share almost 80% of basic words, but have different sounds and different grammar. Both are Huilliche languages and are related to Mapudungun, the language of the much larger Mapuche ethnic community in Chile.

The people of both communities are aware of and alarmed by the severely endangered status of their languages. Among the Choroy Traiguen there are few, if any, speakers of Tsesungun younger than 70 years of age. And among the Wequetrumao there are less than a dozen fluent speakers of Huillichesungun. The youngest speaker, Hugo Antipani, is 40, but all the others are a generation older. The lack of young people fluent in a language greatly endangers it.

People in both communities are saddened about the disappearing languages. While they believe that the languages may soon disappear, they are trying to keep them alive.

In the village of Choroy Traiguen, people use Tsesungun greetings and even some words (such as the words for *mother earth* and *wisdom*) in their everyday Spanish as a way to show that they are proud of their language and their culture and want to keep them alive.

The Enduring Voices team noted that both ethnic and linguistic pride are extremely strong in the Wequetrumao community. A kindergarten in the Wequetrumao village teaches children the basics of the language and culture. And two young hip-hop performers have written song lyrics that include words in Huillichesungun.

Huilliche language activist Anselmo Nuyado Ancapichun said that language is important because it "gives access to other ways of thinking, helps combat acculturation, perpetuates cultural values, and unites the people."

A Circle the correct word to complete the sentences.

1. The Huilliche community is located in Chile / Argentina.
2. The vocabulary of the Tsesungun and Huillichesungun languages is very similar / different.
3. The endangered languages have few / many fluent speakers.
4. The youngest / oldest speaker of Huillichesungun is 40 years old.
5. Some Choroy Traiguen / Wequetrumao use Tsesungun greetings and words in their conversations.

B Choose the best restatement of the given sentence.

1. There are actually two distinct languages spoken by the Huilliche community.
   a. The Huilliche community includes people that speak a dying language.
   b. The Huilliche community includes people that speak two different languages.
   c. Most people in the Huilliche community speak Spanish.
2. The two languages share almost 80% of basic words, but have different sounds and different grammar.
   a. If a person speaks one language he or she can understand the other.
   b. The languages have the same verb forms.
   c. The vocabulary is similar but the grammar is not, and the languages sound different.
3. The youngest speaker is 40, but all the others are a generation older.
   a. Most speakers of the language are at least 60 years old.
   b. The parents of the 40-year-old do not speak the language.
   c. The older generation speaks Spanish.

OUTCOME MET: work with restatement questions

C If you were part of the Enduring Voices team and wanted to know more about the Huilliche community, what would you ask them? Write six thoughtful interview questions.

1. ______________________________

2. ______________________________

3. ______________________________

4. ______________________________

5. ______________________________

6. ______________________________

Outcomes

A Write three sentences about your classmates using the quantifiers in parentheses.

Example: (all) All students in my class speak English.

1. (either) ______
2. (quite a few) ______
3. (none) ______

How did you do?: On a scale of 1–5 (5 being the best), how well did you **use quantifiers to talk about amounts?** ______

B Write what you would say directly to the people in these situations.

1. A friend invites you to meet at a cafe. She never has any money and you always have to pay for her. ______
2. A classmate who copied his term paper from the Internet got a good grade. ______
3. You don't like your sister's new friend because she is rude. ______

How did you do?: On a scale of 1–5, how well did you **bring up negative and sensitive topics?** ______

C Read the restated sentence and then write the original sentence from the reading on page 4.

1. They know about and are concerned about the disappearing languages. ______
2. There are less than twelve Wequetrumao people that speak Huillichesungun fluently. ______
3. The Wequetrumao are very proud of their culture and language. ______

How did you do?: On a scale of 1–5, how well did you **work with restatement questions?** ______

D Read the report about communication and media in Bhutan and answer the questions.

In Bhutan happiness and tradition are very important and money and modern technology is less important. A report says 28% of families have a television, 11% of families own cell phones, 3% have a computer. There is a national TV network and some radio stations. There are three newspapers.

1. What does this report tell you about the people of Bhutan? ______
2. Is this report true for your country? Why or why not? ______
3. Is the information in the last two sentences of the report important? Explain. ______

How did you do?: On a scale of 1–5, how well did you **interpret and question the results of a report?** ______

2 Money Talks

Vocabulary and Grammar

Unit 2 Outcomes

- describe spending habits and preferences
- use noun clauses to explain thoughts in more detail
- determine the meaning of unfamiliar words in a text
- consider the advantages and disadvantages of something

A Match each word or phrase to the correct meaning.

1. ___ loan	a. careful with money
2. ___ materialistic	b. money that you owe
3. ___ save up	c. the money remaining after your bills are paid
4. ___ pay back	d. a plan that shows the amount of money available to spend
5. ___ value	e. money you borrow or lend
6. ___ debt	f. return the money you owe
7. ___ affluent	g. put money aside for future use
8. ___ thrifty	h. valuing money and possessions very highly
9. ___ disposable income	i. wealthy
10. ___ budget	j. attach importance to something

B Circle the correct word to complete the sentences.

1. I wonder how / that much money I need to save.
2. Tony thinks where / that he will splurge on a new laptop.
3. They don't know how she can / can she afford such a nice apartment.
4. Diane told me that / how much the new TV cost.
5. She doesn't know how much / how to pay the money back.
6. He understands why / where people buy expensive cars.

OUTCOME MET: use noun clauses to explain thoughts in more detail

C Change the questions to statements that use noun clauses.

Example: How do affluent people spend their money? *I wonder how affluent people spend their money.*

1. Who splurges on their birthday?

   ____

2. Why does your brother value this old bicycle?

   ____

3. How does she spend her disposable income?

   ____

4. Why is she so thrifty?

   ____

5. What is he saving up for?

____

6. When will the students pay back their loans?

____

OUTCOME MET: use noun clauses to explain thoughts in more detail

D Write a paragraph describing a big purchase that you would like to make. How would you accomplish the purchase? Use at least five words from the box in your paragraph.

budget	**debt**	**loan**	**sacrifice**	**splurge**
credit	**disposable income**	**pay back**	**save up**	**thrifty**

____
____
____
____
____
____

OUTCOME MET: describe spending habits and preferences

Video

A Watch the video and check (✓) *True* or *False*. Then correct the false sentences.

	True	False
1. Sometimes borrowing money can help us accomplish a goal.	☐	☐
2. Financial institutions can't help you purchase a car.	☐	☐
3. Interest is paid at the end of the loan term.	☐	☐
4. All loans have the same interest rate and time frame.	☐	☐
5. A bank may charge fees for late payments on a loan.	☐	☐

B Answer the questions about the video with complete sentences.

1. When is it a good idea to borrow money from a bank? ______________________________

2. What does APR stand for and what does it mean? ______________________________

3. What should you pay attention to before you take a loan from a bank? ______________________________

Writing

A There are different ways to pay for things. Which do you prefer? Write words and phrases to describe the pictures.

B Make a list of pros and cons of paying by cash. Now make another list of pros and cons of paying by credit card.

Cash	
Pros	**Cons**

Credit Card	
Pros	**Cons**

C Now imagine that your family is going to buy something expensive for the home such as a new refrigerator or television. Decide how they should pay: cash or credit card. Then explain the advantages and disadvantages of that method of payment.

OUTCOME MET: consider the advantages and disadvantages of something

Reading

The Real Price of Gold

Gold has great cultural significance in India. Some call it an obsession.[1] The country produces very little gold, but demand is high. India has had the highest demand for gold in the world for several decades. (China has the second highest, and the United States the third.) Some gold is kept in the country's central bank, but India's citizens possess most of the gold. They use it on special occasions and as their savings.

For many Indians, gold plays an important part in major life events. "We grow up in an atmosphere of gold," says Renjith Leen, a news magazine editor in Cochin, a major port city in the state of Kerala.

When a baby is born in Kerala, a grandmother rubs a gold coin in honey and places a drop of the liquid on the baby's tongue for good luck. Over the next six months, the baby receives gifts of gold jewelry on special occasions. These occasions include baptism[2] and the first time he or she eats solid food. Then, when the child is three years old, a family member takes a gold coin and traces words on the child's tongue so that the child will speak beautifully.

"It's written into our DNA,"[3] says K. A. Babu, a manager at a jewelry store in Cochin. "Gold equals good fortune."

Gold is an important part of almost all of the ten million weddings that take place in India every year for two reasons. First, for its beauty. Gold is woven into clothing and made into jewelry that is worn in the wedding ceremonies. Second, for its value. It is an important tradition for the bride's family to give the groom's family some amount of gold among other gifts.

Gold is also very important to the Indian economy. "Gold is the basis of our financial system," says Babu, the jewelry store manager. "People see it as the best form of security, and nothing else lets you get cash as quickly."

Keeping, rather than selling, gold is an ancient tradition for many families in India. But there is also a tradition of pawning gold. Sometimes, when people need money quickly or for an emergency, they pawn gold jewelry and plan to buy it back. Pawning jewelry is different than simply selling it because the seller can buy back the jewelry if he or she pays back the loan on time.

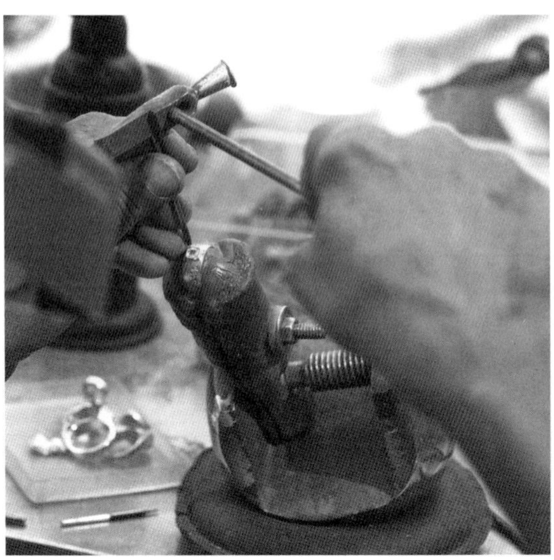

Some people pawn their jewelry at commercial banks while others go to a pawnbroker, a person who buys gold and holds it until the seller can buy it back. The interest rates on loans from pawned jewelry are usually very high.

George Varghese, a pawnbroker in Kerala, says that he handles around half a million dollars in pawned gold each month and even more during harvest and wedding seasons. Varghese says that almost everyone buys back their gold jewelry. Most Indians don't want to let go of their gold. "Even when gold hit $1,000 an ounce, nobody sold their jewelry or coins," says Varghese. "This is their nest egg, and they trust it to keep growing."

[1] **obsession** something people spend a lot of or too much time thinking about
[2] **baptism** ceremony in which a person becomes a member of a church
[3] **written into our DNA** something that is common to all people of a certain group or family. In this case it refers to Indians.

A Choose the meaning of the underlined word(s).

1. Gold has great cultural significance in India.
   a. decoration b. importance c. official
2. India has had the highest demand for gold for several decades.
   a. amount of something wanted b. amount of something produced c. amount of something made
3. We grow up in an atmosphere of gold.
   a. living in b. surrounded by c. wearing a lot of
4. Gold is the basis of our financial system.
   a. currency b. wealth c. foundation
5. Some people pawn their jewelry at commercial banks.
   a. for public benefit b. for profit c. run by the government
6. This is their nest egg, and they trust it to keep growing.
   a. savings b. debt c. interest payments

OUTCOME MET: determine the meaning of unfamiliar words in a text

B Answer the questions about the reading.

1. What is the main idea of the reading? ____________________
2. How is gold used with babies? ____________________
3. What are two ways gold is used in weddings in India? ____________________
4. Why is gold important to India's economy? ____________________
5. How can people get money for their gold jewelry? ____________________

C When people in India need money they often pawn their gold jewelry. Write a paragraph describing the advantages and disadvantages of doing this.

____

OUTCOME MET: consider the advantages and disadvantages of something

Outcomes

A Answer the following questions based on your personal experience.

1. What do you do with your disposable income? ______
2. Are you saving up for anything? Explain. ______
3. Do you buy things on credit? Why or why not? ______

How did you do?: On a scale of 1–5 (with 5 being the best), how well did you **describe spending habits and preferences?** ______

B Change each question about Indian spending habits and preferences into a noun clause.

1. How do many Indians get money when they need it? ______
2. Where can people go to pawn gold? ______
3. What is the risk of pawning gold? ______

How did you do?: On a scale of 1–5, how well did you **use noun clauses to explain thoughts in more detail?** ______

C Write a definition for the words in bold.

1. The **surplus** of housing has caused home prices to fall.
2. The bank **refunded** my account when I showed them the charge was a mistake.
3. Real estate in the city is a wise **investment** right now and sure to increase in value.

How did you do?: On a scale of 1–5, how well did you **determine the meaning of unfamiliar words in a text?** ______

D Write a paragraph on the advantages and disadvantages of the way you currently manage your money.

How did you do?: On a scale of 1–5, how well did you **consider the advantages and disadvantages of something?** ______

3 Bright Lights, Big Cities

Vocabulary and Grammar

Unit 3 Outcomes

- express actions and conditions in the passive voice
- use an outline to summarize
- use statistics to understand a writer's point of view
- write a summary

A Complete the paragraph with the correct vocabulary words. One word is used twice, and three words will not be used.

chaotic	cosmopolitan	district	global	inhabitants	manageable
community	descendants	dynamic	immigrants	livable	metropolitan

In Northern Patagonia, Chile, many people are (1) ________ of German settlers. This (2) ________ is referred to as the German Chileans. These (3) ________ continue to live in the same region as their distant relatives, who came as (4) ________ more than 150 years ago. At that time the (5) ________ was forestland. Most of the German settlers cleared the land for farming and made the area (6) ________. Others went to live in (7) ________ areas including Valdivia and the (8) ________ seaport city of Valparaiso. But they were not the only Europeans there. Valparaiso became a (9) ________ city because the busy port brought many visitors and (10) ________.

B Circle *correct* or *incorrect* for the underlined verb(s) in passive voice. If the passive voice verb(s) are incorrect, rewrite them.

1. Valparaiso <u>was built</u> on steep hills by early settlers. correct / incorrect ________
2. If you <u>acquaint</u> with the city, you know about the funicular[1] elevators people ride up the hills. correct / incorrect ________
3. The hillsides <u>are crowd</u> with colorful houses. correct / incorrect ________
4. Besides culture and tourism, the city <u>is associated</u> with shipping, the navy, and the congress. correct / incorrect ________
5. The National Congress of Chile <u>was move</u> to Valparaiso from the capital Santiago in 1990. correct / incorrect ________

C Answer the questions with complete sentences.

1. Do you live in a large **metropolitan** area or a small **community**? Explain. ________
2. Is public transportation in your city or town **manageable**? ________
3. What factors make your city or town **livable**? ________
4. What **communities** or **districts** is your city or town known for? ________

[1] **funicular** a cable railway that goes up a very steep hill

D Use the word prompts to write sentences. Use the dynamic passive in sentences 1–3. Use the stative passive in sentences 4–6.

Example: New York City / known / the Big Apple *New York City is known as the Big Apple.*

1. scholarships / award / students ______________________
2. statue / move / location ______________________
3. Web site / create / students ______________________
4. city / fill / parks ______________________
5. children / dress / costumes ______________________
6. museum / crowd / tourists ______________________

OUTCOME MET: express actions and conditions in the passive voice

E Use the word prompts to write sentences in the dynamic passive or stative passive. You may change the order of the words in the prompt.

Example: involve / community *The Greek community was involved in planning the festival.*

1. crowd / district ______________________
2. know / cosmopolitan ______________________
3. establish / immigrants ______________________
4. build / dynamic ______________________
5. situate / metropolitan ______________________
6. make / descendants ______________________

OUTCOME MET: express actions and conditions in the passive voice

Video

A Answer the questions with complete sentences according to the video.

1. How many years has it taken for Ulan Bator's population to double?

   ____

2. Why has Namdag moved from the steppe to the city?

   ____

3. What has caused the extreme weather in Mongolia?

   ____

4. What is a possible consequence of the lack of rain and snow in Mongolia?

   ____

5. What does Basanjav want his children and grandchildren to do?

   ____

B In your own words, write a summary of the video on a separate piece of paper.

OUTCOME MET: write a summary

Writing

A Read *Green in the City* on page 16. Underline the main idea of the reading and the three supporting points.

B Complete an outline for the reading starting with the main idea and supporting points from Exercise **A**. Then give examples that reinforce the supporting points. Use note form (do not write complete sentences).

I. green spaces make cities livable and people healthy
II. trees and plants filter air
    A. (1) ____________________
III. (2) ____________________
    A. (3) ____________________
IV. (4) ____________________
    A. (5) ____________________
    B. people were also less aggressive / violent and felt safer

C Write a summary of the reading in your own words using your outline in Exercise **B**.

____
____
____
____
____
____

OUTCOMES MET: use an outline to summarize; write a summary

Reading

Green in the City

In a busy metropolitan area it can be hard to find green space or a park. While many cities have parks and gardens, they are not in every district. But they should be. New research shows that green spaces make cities more livable and can help people stay healthier. This is important because half of the world's population lives in cities. Frances Kuo studies the effects of green space on people who live in cities. "Without access to grass and trees," she says, "we humans are very different creatures."

Scientific research shows that trees and plants filter pollution in the air and trap tiny particles of dirt and soot. For example, trees along a street can reduce the amount of pollution from car and bus exhaust. And the more trees in an area, the better. In Chicago, scientists found that each year trees removed some 234 tons of particles, 98 tons of nitrogen dioxide, 93 tons of sulfur dioxide, and 17 tons of carbon monoxide from the air.

Trees also provide shade, which cools the heat given off by streets and sidewalks. The temperature of asphalt or concrete under a shade tree can be as much as 36°F (20°C) cooler than pavement in full summer sun.

Finally, parks and gardens are very important to people's social and psychological well-being. Kuo and her colleagues studied Chicago's public housing neighborhoods, where some high-rise buildings were surrounded by grass and trees, others by concrete and asphalt. The team discovered that people living in buildings near green areas had a stronger sense of community and coped better with everyday stress and problems than people living without any green space. Also, they were less aggressive and less violent, and felt safer when surrounded by green space. The greener the surroundings, says Kuo, the lower the crime rate against people and property. The team also found less litter and graffiti in natural landscapes.

Cities are dynamic and chaotic. Being close to nature in urban areas may be more important than ever to make city living manageable for inhabitants. Parks can help people stay physically healthy and avoid health problems like obesity and diabetes. Two big recent studies of people in metropolitan areas in the Netherlands and Japan showed that people living in areas close to green spaces where they could walk had better health and lower death rates than people living far from green spaces. Health studies suggest that almost any contact with nature lowers blood pressure and anxiety levels.

"Parks help people take care of themselves so cities don't have to spend as much on social, medical, and safety services trying to fix their problems," says Kuo.

A Choose the best answers according to the reading.

1. ____________ of the world's population live in cities.
   a. 40% b. 50% c. 60%
2. In Chicago trees removed ____________ of carbon monoxide from the air.
   a. 234 tons b. 93 tons c. 17 tons
3. The temperature of the sidewalk under a shade tree can be up to ____________ cooler than the sidewalk in the sun.
   a. 16°F b. 45°F c. 36°F
4. One researcher says that the crime rate is ____________ in green surroundings.
   a. lower b. higher c. increasing
5. Two studies showed that people living near green spaces had lower ____________ rates.
   a. diabetes b. death c. heart

B Answer the questions about the reading.

1. Based on the statistics in Exercise **A**, what is the writer's point of view (positive, negative, or neutral)?

   ____

   ____

2. What inferences can you make about the city of Chicago?

   ____

   ____

3. Based on the reading, do you think cities will increase the number of urban green spaces? Why or why not?

   ____

   ____

4. Do you agree with the idea that green spaces could save society money? Why or why not?

   ____

   ____

OUTCOME MET: use statistics to understand a writer's point of view

C Imagine that you work for your city or town. Write a paragraph to persuade it to plant more trees and create more green spaces.

____

____

____

____

____

____

____

____

____

____

Outcomes

A Answer the questions based on your own experience. Use the verb in parentheses in either the dynamic or stative passive.

1. How old is your house / apartment? (built) ______________________________

____

2. What is special about your city or town? (know) ______________________________

____

How did you do?: On a scale of 1–5 (with 5 being the best), how well did you **express actions and conditions in the passive voice?** _____

B Complete the outline about the nomads in Mongolia based on the video.

I. More Mongolians are leaving the plains and (1) ______________________________

II. Life on the steppe has become hard because of (2) ______________________________ caused by (3) ______________________________

III. The heat and drought have (4) ______________________________

How did you do?: On a scale of 1–5, how well did you **use an outline to summarize?** _____

C Newville is a city of 1.5 million people that has recently received 100,000 new people who are looking for work. About 60% of those people have been unable to find jobs and are using the city's social services. To help them, the mayor is proposing a 1% tax increase, which would help 25,000 people train for and find jobs within eighteen months.

What is the writer's point of view on the situation in Newville? How are the statistics used to support this point of view?

____

____

____

____

____

How did you do?: On a scale of 1–5, how well did you **use statistics to understand a writer's point of view?** _____

D Write a brief summary about the nomads in Mongolia based on the video. Use the outline in Exercise **B** to help you.

____

____

____

____

How did you do?: On a scale of 1–5, how well did you **write a summary?** _____

1–3 Review

Vocabulary Review

A Match the word to its definition.

1. ____ affecting all parts of the world		a. value
2. ____ to change		b. adapt
3. ____ able to be dealt with easily		c. debt
4. ____ to attach importance to something		d. possess
5. ____ to change ideas or behavior in order to deal with something successfully		e. inhabitant
6. ____ to have or to own		f. budget
7. ____ a plan that shows the amount of money available to spend		g. manageable
8. ____ a serious argument about something important		h. switch
9. ____ money that you owe		i. global
10. ____ a person who lives in a particular place		j. conflict

B Complete each sentence by providing a definition for the word or phrase.

Example: *Thrifty* means careful with money.

1. *Credit* is ______________________________
2. A *community* is ______________________________
3. *Collaborative* means ______________________________
4. To *pay back* is ______________________________
5. To *splurge* means ______________________________
6. *Sensitive* means ______________________________

C Write four sentences about yourself or people you know. Use at least one different word or expression from the box in each sentence.

affluent	**disposable income**	**impulsive**	**remark**	**save up**
cosmopolitan	**dynamic**	**loan**	**sacrifice**	**whine**

Example: My brother is saving up to buy a car.

1. ______________________________
2. ______________________________
3. ______________________________
4. ______________________________

Grammar Review

A Change each question into a noun clause.

Example: Karina's birthday is Saturday. What should I give her for a gift?
I wonder what I should give her for a gift.

1. Dylan and Amanda had a baby girl. What's her name?
____
2. Andrew doesn't have a job. How can he afford a new car?
____
3. I want to take a vacation. Where should I go?
____
4. Some people ride motorcycles without helmets. Why do they do that?
____
5. There are two new people in the office. Who are they?
____
6. I'd like to see Jacob tonight. When does he get off work?
____

B Choose the correct form of the passive verb to complete the sentence.

1. Cities today _______________ with millions of people.
   a. are crowded b. crowded c. was crowded
2. The capital of the United States _______________ to Washington, DC, in 1800.
   a. move b. is moved c. was moved
3. The subway system in London _______________ as the Tube.
   a. is known b. known c. knew
4. Are you _______________ with the neighborhoods of Bogotá, Colombia?
   a. acquaint b. was acquainted c. acquainted
5. The Brooklyn Bridge _______________ in 1883.
   a. was complete b. was completed c. is completed
6. The city of Guayaquil _______________ on the Guayas River in Ecuador.
   a. situates b. is situated c. is situating

The Brooklyn Bridge.

C Write fives sentences about yourself or someone you know. Use a different quantifier from the box in each sentence.

a few	any	either	many	much

1. _______________
2. _______________
3. _______________
4. _______________
5. _______________

4 Being Yourself

Vocabulary and Grammar

Unit 4 Outcomes

- describe types of personalities
- use *wish* to talk about things you would like, to express regret, and to express displeasure
- compare and contrast your personality with another person's
- describe factors that contribute to happiness and well-being

A Circle the correct word to complete the sentences.

1. Caitlin is reserved / upbeat and rarely says what she thinks.
2. My job is difficult because my manager is sensible / demanding.
3. Ryan is very picky / affectionate and complains about everything.
4. Young professionals are often hardworking and ambitious / supportive.
5. Technology companies usually hire idealistic / innovative people.
6. Danielle is sensible / supportive and makes good decisions.

B Complete the sentences using the correct verb form. You may need to add an auxiliary verb.

1. Tito is afraid of spiders. He wishes he (be) ___________ a little braver.
2. Khaled was lazy and didn't prepare for the test. Now he wishes that he (study) ___________ more.
3. My friend was so stubborn last week. I wish she (listen) ___________ to my advice.
4. Amanda is still single, but she wishes she (be) ___________ married.
5. It's very hot in here. I wish that someone (turn on) ___________ the air conditioner.
6. Courtney forgot to bring her passport. She really wishes she (remember) ___________ to bring it.

C Answer the questions with complete sentences. Use words from the box for ideas.

affectionate	idealistic	pushover	sensible	stubborn	thorough

1. What is your best friend's personality like? ____

____

2. How is your personality like your best friend's? How is it different? ____

____

OUTCOMES MET: describe types of personalities; compare and contrast your personality with another person's

D Read the real situations. Then write the ideal situation using *wish* and the word(s) in parentheses.

Example: Real situation: My cousin is really picky about her food.
Ideal: (be not / stubborn) I wish she weren't so stubborn.

1. Real situation: It's raining.
   Ideal: (be / sunny) ____
2. Real situation: I am very stubborn.
   Ideal: (be / flexible) ____

3. Real situation: The bus is late.
   Ideal: (arrive) ______________________________

4. Real situation: Maria didn't study for the test.
   Ideal: (study / more) ______________________________

5. Real situation: Sam doesn't care about his job.
   Ideal: (be / ambitious) ______________________________

6. Real situation: I don't understand the assignment.
   Ideal: (teacher / explain / again) ______________________________

OUTCOME MET: use *wish* to talk about things you would like, to express regret, and to express displeasure

E What do these types of people wish for? Complete each sentence according to your own experience.

Example: A picky person *wishes that everything were perfect.*

1. A stubborn person ______________________________
2. An ambitious person ______________________________
3. An idealistic person ______________________________
4. What type of person are you? What do you wish for? ______________________________

____

Video

A Watch the video and circle the letter of the correct answer.

1. These people eat a lot of low-calorie food.
   a. Sardinians b. Okinawans c. Seventh-day Adventists
2. Men live as long as women in this place.
   a. Sardinia b. Okinawa c. Loma Linda, California
3. For these people sharing meals with family is very important.
   a. Sardinians b. Okinawans c. Seventh-day Adventists
4. In this culture people have *ikigai*, a reason for which they wake up in the morning.
   a. Sardinians b. Okinawans c. Seventh-day Adventists
5. Among these people longevity is not losing its edge.
   a. Sardinians b. Okinawans c. Seventh-day Adventists

B Answer the questions in complete sentences.

1. How is your lifestyle similar to the lifestyles in the video? How is it different? ______________________________

   ____

2. What do you wish you could do in order to have a healthier lifestyle? ______________________________

   ____

OUTCOMES MET: use *wish* to talk about things you would like, to express regret, and to express displeasure; describe factors that contribute to happiness and well-being

Writing

Imagine that you've placed an ad online for a roommate. Read the two e-mails describing the people who are interested.

Hi, I'm Kenji from Saitama, Japan. I'm 22 years old and just moved here. I am a graphic designer, so I'm working on my computer a lot or taking photos. I play the guitar and like to practice with others. I'm easygoing and friendly. I enjoy meeting new people and going out on the weekends. I hope we can be friends. Also, I smoke . . . but always outside.

Hello, my name is Veronica. I'm from Montreal, Canada, and I'm 24. I've been living here for three years. I work pretty long hours as a secretary at a law firm. So when I get home after a stressful day, I just want to relax. I don't like a lot of noise, and I must have a room with windows. I also have a cat, so I hope that's not a problem.

affectionate	**idealistic**	**reserved**	**supportive**
ambitious	**innovative**	**sensible**	**thorough**
demanding	**pushover**	**stubborn**	**upbeat**

A Describe the two people using words from the box or others you know.

Kenji: ____

Veronica: ____

OUTCOME MET: describe types of personalities

B How is each person like you and different from you? Refer to Exercise **A** and complete the chart.

	Similarities to You	Differences from You
Kenji		
Veronica		

OUTCOME MET: compare and contrast your personality with another person's

C Using the information in Exercises **A** and **B**, write a roommate ad that describes your ideal roommate.

Reading

Stop Food Cravings through Imaginary Eating? Don't eat dessert, just think about it!

Sometimes when people want to lose weight they try not to think about the foods they can't have. But a study suggests that not only thinking about the food, but also imaginary chewing and swallowing of it can reduce cravings.[1]

According to new research, imagining eating a food reduces your interest in that food, so you eat less of it.

When people eat, they react to the food by becoming used to it. The body and mind begin to lose interest. This process is called *habituation*. It explains why the "tenth bite of chocolate, for example, is desired less than the first bite," wrote the study's authors.

The new research is the first to show that habituation can happen by simply thinking about the process of eating the food.

"A lot of people who diet try to avoid thinking about stimuli[2] they crave. This research suggests that may not be the best strategy," said study leader and psychologist Carey Morewedge.

"If you just think about the food itself—how it tastes, smells, and looks—[that will] increase your appetite," Morewedge said.

"This research suggests that it might be better, actually, to force yourself to repeatedly think about tasting, swallowing, and chewing the food you crave to reduce your cravings."

"This works with only the food you've imagined," he added. For instance, imagining eating chocolate would not stop you from eating too much pizza.

The researchers conducted five experiments, all of which showed that people who repeatedly imagined eating chocolate or cheese ate less of it than people who pictured eating the food fewer times, eating a different food, or not eating at all.

One experiment included three groups of people. The first group was told to imagine inserting thirty quarters into a washing machine—which requires the same physical movements as eating M&M's[3]—and then imagine eating just three M&M's. A second group was asked to imagine inserting three quarters into a laundry machine and then imagine eating thirty M&M's. A third group imagined just inserting thirty-three quarters into a laundry machine—without any M&M's.

Each group was then allowed to eat freely from bowls containing 1.5 ounces (40 grams) of M&M's each. When each group said they were done, the bowls were taken away and weighed.

The results showed that the second group, which imagined eating thirty M&M's each, ate fewer of the candies than the two other groups, who imagined eating less.

How much a person eats seems to be much more than a full feeling after a meal. Thinking about eating plays a role as well. Eating less can be easier than you imagined!

[1] **craving** a feeling that you want something very much
[2] **stimuli** something that causes a reaction
[3] **M&M's** chocolate candies with a colorful candy shell

A Check (✓) *True* or *False*. Then correct the false sentences.

	True	False
1. Imagining chewing and swallowing a food again and again increases cravings. ________________	☐	☐
2. *Habituation* happens when the body becomes used to something. ________________	☐	☐
3. Thinking about how food smells and tastes increases your appetite. ________________	☐	☐
4. If you imagine chewing and swallowing pasta over and over again, you won't crave ice cream either. ________________	☐	☐
5. The group that imagined eating thirty M&M's actually ate the fewest. ________________	☐	☐

B Match the words from the reading with their meanings. One meaning will not be used.

1. ____ craving
2. ____ reduce
3. ____ stimuli
4. ____ appetite
5. ____ repeatedly

a. over and over
b. something that causes a response
c. intense desire for something
d. occasionally
e. decrease
f. desire to eat

C In addition to stopping food cravings, how else could this research improve people's happiness and well-being? Write a paragraph describing another way people could use their imagination to help themselves.

____

____

____

____

____

____

____

____

____

____

____

____

____

____

____

OUTCOME MET: describe factors that contribute to happiness and well-being

Outcomes

A Which types of personalities do your family members have? Do you get along with them? Why or why not? Describe at least two.

____

____

____

____

____

How did you do?: On a scale of 1–5 (with 5 being the best), how well did you **describe types of personalities**? ____

B Use the information below to write sentences using *wish*.

1. You are forgetful. ______________________
2. You were late to a meeting yesterday. ______________________
3. Your friend is always borrowing your computer. ______________________

How did you do?: On a scale of 1–5, how well did you **use *wish* to talk about things you would like, to express regret, and to express displeasure**? ____

C Choose a classmate and compare and contrast his / her personality with yours.

____

____

____

____

____

How did you do?: On a scale of 1–5, how well did you **compare and contrast your personality with another person's**? ____

D Answer the questions about cultures of longevity, according to the video.

1. How is family and food important to the Sardinians?

   ____

2. What activities do the older Okinawans do?

   ____

3. What are some of the healthy habits of the Seventh-day Adventists?

   ____

How did you do?: On a scale of 1–5, how well did you **describe factors that contribute to happiness and well-being**? ____

5 Mystery Solved!

Vocabulary and Grammar

Unit 5 Outcomes

- use modals of possibility in the past, present, and future
- speculate about mysteries
- refute ideas
- use *wh-* questions to help you plan a story

A Circle the correct word to complete the sentence.

1. Martin noticed something different about his surroundings / observation.
2. It took a few moments for him to reduce / absorb the situation.
3. He stood quietly at the door of his house and made some remarks / observations.
4. The mystery / theory was: Who opened the door to his house while he was at work?
5. Martin did not enter his home for fear that an aggressive / affectionate person was inside.
6. Instead he called the police to investigate the district / case.

B Choose the correct modal to complete the sentence.

1. "I hear sirens. The police ____________ be on their way," said Martin's neighbor.
   a. could b. must c. must have
2. "I ____________ understand what happened," said Martin.
   a. can't b. could c. must
3. "I ____________ locked the door this morning. I always do," he said.
   a. must b. must have c. couldn't have
4. "You can't enter your house because someone ____________ be in there," the police officer said.
   a. couldn't b. must c. may
5. "We will search inside where we ____________ find some clues," the police officer told Martin.
   a. can't b. might c. must
6. "I ____________ left the door open this morning, could I?" Martin asked himself.
   a. must have b. can't c. couldn't have

OUTCOME MET: use modals of possibility in the past, present, and future

C Answer the questions with complete sentences.

1. What do you think happened at Martin's house? ____________
   ____
2. What theories do you have about a famous mystery, such as an unsolved crime, an ancient monument, or an unexplained phenomenon? Explain your idea(s). ____________
   ____

OUTCOME MET: speculate about mysteries

D Use the prompts to write responses with modals of possibility.

Example: I didn't receive an e-mail from Megan.
(weaker certainty): *You might have told her the wrong e-mail address.*

1. What caused the car accident?
   (strong certainty): ______________________________
2. How is your new job?
   (impossibility): ______________________________
3. I can't find my keys anywhere!
   (strong certainty): ______________________________
4. Our teacher is not here yet.
   (weaker certainty): ______________________________
5. He told me not to call him again.
   (impossibility): ______________________________

OUTCOME MET: use modals of possibility in the past, present, and future

E Imagine that some strange events occurred last night when the power went out. On a separate piece of paper, write an entry in your blog describing the strange events and the possible causes of the events using modals of possibility and words from the box.

case	**observation**
cemetery	**solve**
clue	**theory**
mystery	**uncover**

OUTCOMES MET: use modals of possibility in the past, present, and future; speculate about mysteries

Video

A Watch the video and check (✓) *True* or *False*. Then correct the false sentences.

	True	False
1. Stonehenge is an ancient monument in England. ______________________________	☐	☐
2. Pearson believes that his team has found the settlement where the people who built Stonehenge lived. ______________________________	☐	☐
3. Durrington Walls was a small community with less than one hundred homes. ______________________________	☐	☐
4. The wood structures were for the living and the stone structures were for the dead. ______________________________	☐	☐
5. Stonehenge was not a cemetery according to Pearson. ______________________________	☐	☐

B Answer the questions based on the video. Use modals of possibility in your answers.

1. What do you think about Pearson's theory that Stonehenge was part of a larger complex on Salisbury Plain?
   ____
2. How important is it to try to solve mysteries about ancient structures?
   ____

Writing

A Choose one of the photos and write down as many words as you can to describe what you see.

B Think of a story that explains the mystery in your photo. Make notes about the main details of the story for each *wh-* word. Use some of the words from Exercise **A**.

1. Who?
2. What?
3. When?
4. Where?
5. Why?
6. How?

OUTCOME MET: use *wh-* questions to help you plan a story

C Now imagine that you are making a documentary film about the mystery. Tell your story using the details from Exercise **B**.

OUTCOME MET: speculate about mysteries

Reading

Lost at Sea

On March 7, 1533, a trading ship named the *Bom Jesus*—the *Good Jesus*—set sail from Portugal. It was sailing to India for spices. But it never arrived. And no one knows exactly what happened.

The ship was lost for almost five hundred years. Then, in 2008, a copper ingot[1] was found on a beach in Namibia, Africa. The ingot was the type that Europeans traded for spices in India in the first half of the sixteenth century.

This one copper ingot led archaeologists to a sunken ship 20 feet below sea level, where they found 22 tons of these ingots beneath the sand.

"If it hadn't been for those copper ingots weighing everything down, there would be nothing left here to find," says Bruno Werz, director of the Southern African Institute of Maritime Archaeology. "Five centuries of storms and waves would have washed everything away."

These ingots were a clue to the ship's identity and voyage. The great quantity of ingots suggests the ship was on its way to India to trade for spices rather than returning to Portugal.

There were also more than two thousand heavy gold coins. One special coin, the portugueses, was a clue that helped archaeologists solve another piece of the mystery. The archaeologists had a theory that the ship was Portuguese and must have sailed between 1525 and 1538, because that was when the portugueses were minted, and many were found in the shipwreck.

Portuguese shipping records show that twenty-one ships were lost between 1525 and 1600, but only one ship disappeared near Namibia—the *Bom Jesus*, which sailed in 1533 and was "lost on the turn of the Cape of Good Hope."

One theory says that the ship may have encountered a huge storm as it was sailing around the cape. In the aftermath the ship may have gotten lost and far off course. A further theory speculates that strong winds and ocean currents could have driven the ship hundreds of miles toward the coast, where it eventually hit rocks and sank.

Did anyone survive? Archaeologists uncovered the bones of only one person in the shipwreck. Also very few personal possessions were found among the artifacts. These details led archaeologists to believe that nearly everyone on the ship made it to land.

And then what? The coast is sandy with little vegetation, but there is a river only 16 miles away. The survivors could have eaten shellfish, seabird eggs, and desert snails. People who would have been living in this part of Africa in 1533 were hunter-gatherers. Perhaps they taught the Portuguese how to survive. But that is still a mystery.

[1] **ingot** metal made into a shape that is easy for transport, such as gold bars

A Underline the theories described in the reading.

B Match the place to its description based on the reading.

1. ____ The destination of the *Bom Jesus*.
2. ____ The place where the *Bom Jesus* got lost.
3. ____ The place from which the *Bom Jesus* set sail.
4. ____ The place near the shipwreck of the *Bom Jesus*.

a. Portugal
b. India
c. Namibia
d. the Cape of Good Hope

C Answer the questions with your own ideas.

1. The article says that few personal possessions were found in the shipwreck. Why is this clue important to the theory that there could have been survivors?

   ____

   ____

2. What inferences can you make about the Cape of Good Hope based on the article?

   ____

   ____

3. How was trade in the 1500s different than today?

   ____

   ____

D One theory presented in the article is that most people on the *Bom Jesus* survived the shipwreck and made it to land. Write a paragraph that refutes this theory using modals of possibility and phrases such as *It seems unlikely that . . .* and *I doubt that . . .* (see Student Book, page 54).

____

____

____

____

____

____

____

____

____

____

____

____

____

OUTCOMES MET: use modals of possibility in the past, present, and future; refute ideas

Outcomes

A Respond to the situations using modals of possibility.

1. My cell phone won't work. ______
2. Joshua said he didn't hear the phone ring. ______
3. I finally found my keys! ______

How did you do?: On a scale of 1–5 (with 5 being the best), how well did you **use modals of possibility in the past, present, and future**? ______

B The article about the *Bom Jesus* says that twenty-one Portuguese ships were lost at sea between 1525 and 1600. Write a paragraph explaining what could have happened to these ships.

______

How did you do?: On a scale of 1–5, how well did you **speculate about mysteries**? ______

C Refute the statements with complete sentences.

1. The *Bom Jesus* was attacked by pirates. ______
2. Stonehenge was created by aliens. ______
3. Crop circles are a man-made phenomenon. ______

How did you do?: On a scale of 1–5, how well did you **refute ideas**? ______

D Imagine that you are going to write a story about the survivors of the *Bom Jesus*. Answer the *wh-* questions to help you think of the main details of the story.

1. What happened to the survivors? ______
2. Where did it happen? ______
3. How did they survive? ______
4. Why didn't anyone know about it? ______

How did you do?: On a scale of 1–5, how well did you **use *wh-* questions to help you plan a story**? ______

6 New Horizons

Vocabulary and Grammar

Unit 6 Outcomes

- make predictions using different future forms
- identify key words used to explain reasons
- describe skills needed to achieve future goals
- develop and write a counterargument

A Match the words or phrases with their meanings.

1. ___ primitive	a. able to do tasks successfully, without wasting time or energy
2. ___ inspire	b. good enough for people to live in
3. ___ efficient	c. no longer necessary because something better has been invented
4. ___ versatile	d. able to be used for many different purposes
5. ___ habitable	e. to encourage or make someone want to do something
6. ___ take (something) for granted	f. possible
7. ___ obsolete	g. the most advanced or most exciting in a particular field
8. ___ cutting-edge	h. to communicate as you work or spend time with others
9. ___ interact (with)	i. accept that something is true or normal without thinking about it
10. ___ feasible	j. simple; not well developed

B Choose the correct future form for each sentence.

1. By 2100 sea levels ____________________ significantly.
   a. were going to rise b. will have risen c. would rise
2. David knew that hiring more people ____________________ his job easier.
   a. will be making b. will have made c. would make
3. After just a few months of classes Alma ____________________ English very well.
   a. will be speaking b. will have spoken c. would speak
4. Someday soon computers ____________________ most appliances in our homes.
   a. will be controlling b. will have controlled c. would control
5. In one hour everyone ____________________ the results, so we should prepare an explanation.
   a. will be seeing b. will have seen c. would see
6. Emily thought that learning English ____________________ traveling in Europe easier.
   a. will make b. will have made c. was going to make

C Answer the questions with complete sentences.

1. Some technologies make **interacting with** other people **obsolete**. What are the benefits and **drawbacks** of this?

   ____

   ____

2. Is it important for you to have a **cutting-edge** mobile phone, laptop, or other device? Why or why not?

   ____

   ____

D Write predictions about yourself or people you know using future forms. Use each future form (future continuous, future perfect, and future in the past) at least once.

1. A year from now ______
2. In five years, ______
3. I knew ______
4. By 2020, ______
5. When I'm 50 years old ______

OUTCOME MET: make predictions using different future forms

E Answer the questions in complete sentences using future forms.

1. Which cutting-edge technology will become obsolete in the next five years?
______
2. How will mobile devices be made even more versatile in the future?
______
3. Is it feasible that people will be living on other planets by 2200?
______

Video

A Answer the questions according to the video.

1. What's the most exciting part of Alexandra Cousteau's work as an explorer?
______
______
2. What excited Johan Reinhard the most about finding the Inca mummies?
______
______
3. How did Johan Reinhard know that the mummy's body was frozen?
______
______
4. According to Sylvia Earle, what happens when you spend a lot of time exploring the ocean?
______

B Imagine you are an explorer. Where would you explore? Predict some of the things you will do or discover.

______
______
______
______
______

Writing

Read the article about robots on page 36.

A How does Hiroshi Ishiguro feel about robots and their role in society? Write a summary of his opinion.

B What reason does Ishiguro give for this view? Write his reason and then write one drawback to this reason.

Reason:

Drawback:

C Write a counterargument that argues against Ishiguro's reason in Exercise **B**. Remember to first state the opinion you disagree with, then give your opinion and reason for disagreeing.

OUTCOME MET: develop and write a counterargument

Reading

Robots: Outsourcing to Machines

Androids are being designed to perform tasks in our homes, schools, and offices—tasks that until now have been done exclusively[1] by people. And believe it or not, these versatile robots may be available to you in the near future.

"In five or ten years robots will routinely be functioning in human environments," says Reid Simmons, a professor of robotics at Carnegie Mellon University.

Robots can be helpful with tasks around the house. For example, the Roomba vacuum conveniently moves itself around furniture to keep floors clean. But would you want a robot to prepare your meals? Would you allow a robot to babysit your children or take care of your elderly parents?

Some scientists actually study the interaction between humans and robots. Keep in mind that people will need to adapt themselves in order to interact with robots. Scientists find that people respond positively to robots with a human appearance and movements, but only up to a certain point. As soon as people sense that a robot is too lifelike, their response turns very negative. One of the main reasons for this is because the robots are so close to being real without actually being alive.

One man, Hiroshi Ishiguro, has been involved with the development of many innovative robots, which he uses to explore human–robot interaction. He created a robot that is his own robotic twin. He created the robot so that he could be in two places at once. Ishiguro works in a lab in Kyoto, Japan, and also teaches at Osaka University, which is two hours away. The robot, which has the same hair, same facial expressions, and same clothing as Ishiguro, stays in Kyoto. Using the Internet, Ishiguro controls the robot through motion-capture sensors on its face so that he can interact with his colleagues at the lab while he stays at Osaka to teach.

"You believe I'm real, and you believe that thing is not human," Ishiguro says, pointing to the robot. "But this distinction will become more difficult as the technology advances. If you finally can't tell the difference, does it really matter if you're interacting with a human or a machine?"

An ideal use for his robot-twin, Ishiguro says, would be to put it at the faraway home of his mother, whom he rarely visits, so she could be with him more.

"Why would your mother accept a robot?" I ask.

Two faces scowl[2] back at me. "Because it is myself," says one.

However uncomfortable the facts may be, robots are being created that can and will interact more frequently with humans. As the technology improves, it's likely you will see more and more robots performing human roles, such as caregiving. While most people would not consider a robot their equal, there may come a day when we take it for granted that robots are our equals.

[1] **exclusively** limited to a single individual or group
[2] **scowl** to contract the brow to make an angry or hostile expression

A Underline the key words and phrases used to explain reasons in the article.

OUTCOME MET: identify key words used to explain reasons

B Answer the questions based on the article.

1. What turns people's responses to robots negative?

____

____

2. How does / will Hiroshi Ishiguro's robot twin make life easier for him?

____

____

C Answer the questions with your own ideas.

1. What can you infer about the writer when he asks, "Why would your mother accept a robot?"

____

____

2. What inference can you make about Ishiguro based on his feeling of equality with his robotic twin?

____

____

3. What inference can you make about Ishiguro's relationship with his mother?

____

____

4. What can you infer about the current development of robotics based on the article?

____

____

D Imagine that robots start working in every home in your country. What kind of skills will people need to develop in order to successfully interact with the robots?

____

____

____

____

____

____

____

____

____

____

OUTCOME MET: describe skills needed to achieve future goals

Outcomes

A Write predictions about the subject in parentheses. Use each future form (future continuous, future perfect, and future in the past) once.

1. (a friend) ______
2. (my class) ______
3. (my country) ______

How did you do?: On a scale of 1–5 (with 5 being the best), how well did you **make predictions using different future forms?** ______

B Circle the key words that explain reasons.

1. One of the main reasons / We take it for granted that robots will be used more in the future is because they are more efficient than humans.
2. I knew we would discover / Another reason is that the cost of this cutting-edge technology gets cheaper every year.
3. That said / Keep in mind, robots will not make humans obsolete.

How did you do?: On a scale of 1–5, how well did you **identify key words used to explain reasons?** ______

C Imagine that your job is to make robots more like humans. What skills will you need to achieve this goal?

______
______
______
______
______

How did you do?: On a scale of 1–5, how well did you **describe skills needed to achieve future goals?** ______

D Imagine that your school has decided to replace all English teachers with robots because robots will make language learning more efficient. Write a brief counterargument.

______
______
______
______
______
______

How did you do?: On a scale of 1–5, how well did you **develop and write a counterargument?** ______

4–6 Review

Vocabulary Review

A Complete each sentence with the correct word partnership.

aggressive behavior	**cutting-edge technology**	**energy efficient**	**major drawback**
become obsolete	**demanding schedules**	**familiar surroundings**	**solve mysteries**

1. Detectives search for clues to ______________________.
2. Mobile devices ______________________ very quickly.
3. It's hard to keep up with ______________________ because it's constantly changing.
4. This new refrigerator is so much more ______________________ than our old one.
5. A ______________________ of new technology is the extremely high cost.
6. The students at our university have ______________________ every semester.
7. The dog is showing ______________________, so I think we should back away slowly.
8. After a long business trip overseas, it feels nice to return home to ______________________.

B Circle the word or phrase that does not belong in each group.

1.	aggressive	ambitious	idealistic	observation
2.	get along with	unharmed	take for granted	interact with
3.	efficient	versatile	innovative	primitive
4.	theory	observation	cutting-edge	mystery
5.	reserved	twist	absorb	solve
6.	case	clue	mystery	pushover

C Write sentences about yourself and people you know. In each sentence, use at least one word from the box.

ambitious	**get along (with)**	**interact (with)**	**solve**	**take for granted**
efficient	**idealistic**	**pushover**	**stubborn**	**upbeat**

Example: *My mother gets along well with her sisters.*

1. ______________________
2. ______________________
3. ______________________
4. ______________________

Grammar Review

A **Choose the correct phrase to complete the *wish* statement.**

1. My sister wishes that it ________________ because she likes to ski.
   a. would snow b. snows c. will snow
2. There's so much traffic! I wish that we ________________ the subway.
   a. take b. had taken c. will take
3. Robyn wishes she ________________ wake up so early for work.
   a. won't b. didn't have to c. had
4. I wish that I ________________ more for my driving test.
   a. had practiced b. have practiced c. have been practicing
5. Tania wishes that she ________________ more patient with her students.
   a. is b. were c. was
6. I wish I ________________ travel to the music festival with you.
   a. would b. could c. will

B **Circle the correct modal of possibility to complete the sentence.**

1. Nadia isn't answering, but she must / might have her cell phone with her.
2. My car won't start. I guess I could / could not take the bus to work.
3. Someone sent these beautiful flowers. It couldn't / must be your husband.
4. Here . . . try my bicycle. It might / might not be easier for you to ride.
5. That's impossible! She might / couldn't have gotten the highest score.
6. Let's not use the alarm because it might / must scare away the cat.

C **Complete the sentences using future forms. Use each future form (future continuous, future perfect, and future in the past) at least once.**

1. By the time I am ________________ years old I ________________________________.
2. By the end of the day ____.
3. Five years from now ____.
4. Before my next birthday ____.
5. I thought that ____.
6. (your idea) ____.

Review Surveys

Unit 1: Talking about language

Ask your classmates the following questions. Keep track of their responses in the chart below.

1. Where do you speak English outside of class?
2. When you have a conversation in English and you don't understand something the other person says, what do you do?
3. How do you like to communicate in English: face to face, by e-mail, or by phone?

Name	Question 1	Question 2	Question 3

Unit 2: Save or spend?

Ask your classmates the following questions. Keep track of their responses in the chart below.

1. Are you thrifty?
2. In your opinion, does paying with a credit card have more advantages or disadvantages?
3. Would you rather have a job that you enjoy doing, but doesn't pay well or a job that you don't enjoy, but pays a lot of money?

Name	Question 1	Question 2	Question 3

Unit 3: Where we live

Ask your classmates the following questions. Keep track of their responses in the chart below.

1. What is the largest city you have visited?
2. What is the best thing about big cities?
3. What kind of transportation do you use in your city or town?

Name	Question 1	Question 2	Question 3

Unit 4: Getting along with others

Ask your classmates the following questions. Keep track of their responses in the chart below.

1. How do you describe your personality?
2. Which personality types do you get along with?
3. Which personality types do you not get along with?

Name	Question 1	Question 2	Question 3

Unit 5: Mysteries

Ask your classmates the following questions. Keep track of their responses in the chart below.

1. What is an unsolved mystery that you know about?
2. Do mysteries interest you? Why or why not?
3. Is it worthwhile for archaeologists to study mysteries from the past? Why or why not?

Name	Question 1	Question 2	Question 3

Unit 6: In touch with technology

Ask your classmates the following questions. Keep track of their responses in the chart below.

1. What was the last technology product you bought?
2. What is something you use now that you predict will be obsolete in twenty years?
3. Would you go to a restaurant where the servers are robots? Why or why not?

Name	Question 1	Question 2	Question 3

Survey Result Reports

Record the results of your surveys as summaries. Use the phrases below to help you.

The majority of people ...	**Quite a few people ...**	**Hardly any of the people ...**
Most people ...	**About half of the people ...**	**Almost no one ...**

Unit 1: Talking about language

Unit 2: Save or spend?

Unit 3: Where we live

Unit 4: Getting along with others

Unit 5: Mysteries

Unit 6: In touch with technology

Review Puzzle Units 1–3

ACROSS	DOWN
1. people of later generations	2. London is a ____ city.
3. Perla does not like her job and ____ about it.	4. My grandmother was an ____ from Greece.
6. give something up	5. When you borrow money, you are in ____.
7. done by two or more people working together	7. There is a serious ____ between the two countries.
8. Are you going to pay with cash or ____?	10. If you are very careful with money, you are ____.
9. information and understanding about a subject	11. It is important to be ____ to others.
11. When did you ____ to a new phone?	14. I took a ____ from the bank to buy a car.
12. People have to ____ to changes in the world.	17. Can you please ____ the directions?
13. opposite of *spend*	19. The school has a very small ____ for books.
15. Iceland has about 320,000 ____.	
16. Boston has a large ____ area.	
18. My sister ____ her designer clothes.	
20. When I get paid, I want to ____ on a new coat.	
21. What ____ of the city do you live in?	
22. wealthy	

Review Puzzle Units 4–6

ACROSS

3. Apple makes ____ products.
5. not hurt
7. Voters won't elect a candidate that is too ____.
10. Traveling across the world by car is not ____.
13. act of carefully watching someone or something
15. Use a towel to ____ the water.
17. I can't ____ this math problem.
19. My cousin is very ____ about food.
21. ____ the handle to open the window.
22. That dog bites. It's ____.
23. a formal idea that explains something
24. Animals are always aware of their ____.
25. Monica is quiet and ____.

DOWN

1. Joan is a very ____ worker.
2. a robot that looks human
4. An ____ person wants very much to succeed.
6. something not understood or known about
8. something that helps you find the answer
9. a situation or incident
11. My parents trust me to make ____ decisions.
12. Long lines in airports are a ____ to flying.
14. New technology often becomes ____ quickly.
16. able to be used for different purposes
18. a person who is easily influenced by others
20. The museum displays ____ tools that are more than one thousand years old.